111 Dynamite Ways to
Ace Your Job Interview

111 Dynamite Ways to Ace Your Job Interview

Richard Fein

IMPACT PUBLICATIONS
Manassas Park, VA

Copyright © 1997 by Richard Fein

3 1218 00290 9811

Library of Congress Cataloging-in-Publication Data

Fein, Richard, 1946—
    111 dynamite ways to ace your job interview / Richard
    Fein.
        p.   cm.
    Includes bibliographical references and index.
    ISBN 1-57023-065-X (alk. paper)
    1. Employment interviewing. I. Title.
HF5549.5.I6F46   1997
650.14—dc21   96-44481
                                                            CIP

For information on distribution or quantity discount rates, Tel. 703/361-7300, Fax 703/335-9486, or write to: Sales Department, IMPACT PUBLICATIONS, 9104-N Manassas Drive, Manassas Park, VA 20111-2366. Distributed to the trade by National Book Network, 4720 Boston Way, Suite A, Lanham, MD 20706, Tel. 301/459-8696 or 800/462-6420.

Contents

Acknowledgments

I would like to thank the following individuals, most of whom are human resource professionals, for reading portions of this book's manuscript and sharing their comments with me. Of course, any errors of content, opinion or presentation remain strictly my own, and inclusion on this list does not imply endorsement of this book's contents.

Evelyn J. Andrews	ECC International Corporation
Jeffrey Annis	L. Knife & Son, Inc.
Chris Asmussen	Olan Mills, Inc.
Keith A. Beavers	MSI International
J. B. Bettlinger	Vicorp Restaurants, Inc.
Arleen Ramirez Borysiewicz	The Washington Center for Internships and Academic Seminars
Roberta Boucher	Lawrence Berkeley National Laboratory
Emilie Brennan	Toshiba America Electronic Components, Inc.

Ilene Hecht Brown	Northwestern Memorial Hospital
Susie Buchler	BSG Alliance/IT, Inc.
Charles Canales	LAC/Olive View-UCLA Medical Center
Doug Cogburn	State of Georgia Merit System
Thomas J. Colbert	Paul Revere Insurance Group
Curtis C. Collins	NASA—Johnson Space Center
Vicki Crouch	Harrison Memorial Hospital
Dena Croy	Reading Rehabilitation Hospital
Vicki Crouch	Harrison Memorial Hospital
Nick Dalton	Sigma Chemical Company
Jamie Davis	Children's Hospital
Valerie Davisson	Thorn Americas, Inc.
Mark E. Day	Price Waterhouse
Stephanie DeFelice	Columbia Tulsa Regional Medical Center
Frances Dezendorf	VA Medical Center, Shreveport, LA
Christopher J. Donner	Devereux Glenholme School
Nancy Duerr	American Health Services
Norma Ellis	Nashua Corporation
James Emerson	Emerson Research Company
Mike Faber	Zeller Corporation
John Flato	Cigna Corporation
Linda Fletcher	The Automation Group
Joyce L. Fowler	Synovus Financial Corporation
Maria J. Frias	Guidant Corporation
Mary C. Fricke	Louis Dreyfus Corporation
Bonnie Gauger	Everen Clearing Corporation
Giavonni Gibson	Carolina First Bank
Tess Graham	Simons-Eastern, Inc.
Susan Gubing	Smithtown Schools
Diana Guiou	Maine Yankee Atomic Power Company
James F. Hamelin	ABB C-E Services, Inc.
Gil Hammond	Geupel DeMars, Inc.
Dave Hextell	Quantum Chemical Company
Stephen Hobbs	Biogen, Employment Manager
Ina Hopiak	Boy Scouts of America
James L. Hose	Glendale Federal Bank
Amy Hohulin	Leo Burnett U.S.A.
Bill Ingham	Aspect Telecommunications
David C. James	(Office of) San Diego City Attorney
Daisy M. Jenkins	Hughes Missile Systems Company
Roger Keast	South Coast Air Quality Management District

Bonnie A. Kriescher	Advocate Health Care
Susan K. Lee	Environmental Resources Management, Inc.
Gail T. Lovelace	U.S. General Services Administration
Stuart J. Madison	Information Builders, Inc.
Joseph M. Mangan	Fuller Company
Linda McKee	Honeywell
Dennis J. McMurray	National Cooperative Refinery Association
Jan Moraczewski	Centennial Area Health Education Center
Nieves Olvera, Jr.	Houston Independent School District
David O. Reynolds	Wolf Creek Nuclear Operating Corporation
Reginald A. McQuay	Toronto Dominion Bank
Mary Nissen, PHR	HR Manager, Ascent Solutions, Inc.
Jeff Parke	Vice President, Operations, GLI International
Dennis J. Przywara	CDI Information Services
John P. Pullen	Marathon Oil Company
Susan Purdy	Berkshire Health Systems
Matthew T. Roberts	Thermadyne Holdings Corporation
Steven Runde	Michigan Consolidated Gas Company
Lauren Ryan	National Semiconductor Corporation
John M. Sabol	Cable Express Corporation
Trish Radtke Scarol	Maersk, Inc.
John Schierer	Thomas & Betts
Jane Senger	Corning, HTA
Ellen Shapiro	Shapiro Communications
Frank J. Sharkey	Puget Sound Naval Shipyard
Ruth Shores	Kino Community Hospital
Carol Smith	Lockheed Martin
Sandra B. Smith	Blue Cross/Blue Shield of LA
Gretchen K. Snediker	Victoria's Secret Catalogue
John W. Sporleder	Itron, Inc.
Andrea D. Stephenson	Florida Hospital Association
Mara Strandlund	The University of Chicago
Barbara K. Sturniolo	New Hanover Regional Medical Center
Joni G. Swope	Saint Joseph Hospital & Health Center
Brian Taffe	LAM Research Corporation
Wendy E. Tarmon	RadioShack
Pam Webster	Enterprise Rent-a-Car

Jim Wilson   Sunbeam Corporation
Kevin C. Wilson   Reuben H. Donnelley
Patricia A. Wilus   South Jersey Gas Company
Pam Wyma   Tyndale House Publishers
Georgine Young   Perot Systems Corporation

In addition, I would like to thank my assistant Janice Dagilus, without whom my work life would be impossible; and my publisher Ron Krannich.

                            Richard Fein
                            December 1996

111 Dynamite Ways to
Ace Your Job Interview

1

Successful Interviewing

Most people like to have a good job. It is our ticket to a paycheck and prestige. A job also provides some measure of our self worth. However, most people do not enjoy the process of interviewing required to get a good job. Perhaps you are one of these people: You know how **to do** a good job but not how to **get** one. The unfortunate result for you could be underemployment or even unemployment.

The goal of this book is to make interviewing less stressful and more successful. You will find this book informative and easy to use. The 111 aces it discusses are divided into seven chapters which take you from pre-interview preparation, to the interview itself, and through post interview follow-up and salary negotiations.

This book is designed for the person in career transition, whether voluntary or not. It will also be helpful to people just beginning their careers and those returning to the work force. It assumes that you are a **plausible** candidate for the job you want and focuses on ways to present your case in the best way possible. We do not assume that you are the **perfect** or obvious candidate for the job. In the employment earthquake which is shaking the US labor market, few of us are in the perfect candidate category.

What's In This Book For You?

There are many books about job interviews, some of which are very good. Why is this book going to be helpful to you? First, this book is complete. It covers the range of topics you need to succeed at your interview. That includes pre-interview preparation in attitude and substance. Then there are 50 interview question topics with explanations and sample answers. A separate chapter on questions you **should ask** your interviewer is included. Also, there is interview follow-up including a "lemons to lemonade" approach, evaluating offers and negotiating better compensation. Second, this book is easy to use. Because the book is organized around 111 aces, you get the information you need in small bites which are easy to digest. If you are interested in a specific aspect of interviewing, the right part of the book is easy to find. Third, I give you both reasons and examples for what I recommend. There is nothing between these covers which is left abstract or purely theoretical. Fourth, this book also gives you many examples of **what-not-to-do** so you avoid shooting yourself in the foot.

Aces and Interviews

What does it mean to "ace your job interview?" The ideas and examples presented in this book are like aces in a card game, let's say poker. Having an ace strengthens your hand. It increases your probability of success.

However, an ace doesn't **guarantee** you will win the game. After all, there are other players in the game, and they may have even more aces or play their hand better than you do. In addition, the judgement of the interviewer, including his/her subjective feelings and personal preferences, is a critical part of the game. The goal of this book then is to **maximize your probability** of winning at your job interview by giving you a handful of aces and an understanding of how to play them. There is no magic formula which will guarantee success.

How Important Is the Health of the US Economy?

Depending on who we listen to, the US economy is either the robust job-creating envy of the world or a changing, downsizing force which is crushing the middle class hopes of millions of Americans. As citizens and human beings we may be deeply concerned about this issue. However, in terms of our individual job search the state of the economy is irrelevant. There is no sense in allowing what you can't influence—the state of the economy—to drain your energy. Instead focus on what you can actively control, namely your attitude and job search skills. Over 115 million Americans are working and many of these people are happy with what they do and what they are paid. This book can help you be one of those fully-employed Americans whether the economy is boom or bust.

Are There Still Jobs?

The classical perception of what a job is has changed. At one time a specific job implied a set of defined tasks. Your public accountant performed audits and the blacksmith made horseshoes. Today your accountant is becoming more of a business consultant and the erstwhile blacksmith may be a combination of automobile parts distributor and auto repair expert. One of the objectives of this book is to show you how to relate your positive characteristics—your skills and attributes—to the needs of your next employer even if the job and industry are different from your past experience.

Is It a Buyer's Market?

I was a guest one evening on a popular radio talk show discussing one of my previous books. The show's host was exceptionally bright and perceptive, but we disagreed on several issues. One was my contention that a job interview is a business meeting between equals.

The host took sharp exception and said "It's a buyers market out there. There are hundreds of applicants for each job." This is a common perception, but I think it is inaccurate and counterproductive. First, you want a job, or at least a new job, but the company also wants something—a new employee. That's why the interview is being held. You might say, "But look at the numbers. There are many applicants for each job." These numbers are misleading for two reasons.

1. Each job may attract a hundred applicants, but each applicant may also seek a hundred jobs.

2. The firm is looking for the **best possible** employee for its needs, within the constraints of what it is willing to pay. Among the hundred applicants in our example, only a few will be candidates for the "best possible" and many of them will have other employment options. What's more, hiring the **wrong** candidate can carry significant costs to the company in terms of employee morale, customer relations and missed opportunities.

The upshot is that the labor market is difficult for both sides of the interview process. Hopefully, you are one of the applicants with the necessary skills and behaviors. This book will show you how to present them in the most positive manner possible.

One further note: The notion of buyer's market (or seller's market) applies best when the product is **undifferentiated**, like bushels of wheat. But people, particularly at a professional level, are very differentiated in terms critical to the employer, like job skills, personal attributes and motivation. This book will help you convince an interviewer that you are the best applicant for the job and not just a non-descript bushel of wheat.

Two Interview Principles

A Business Meeting Between Equals

As a general rule, an interview is a business meeting between equals. You need a new job, the firm needs a new employee.

There are exceptions to this general rule. If you are interviewing for the one and only job that will make you happy, you put yourself at a disadvantage. If your personal situation demands that you get a new job and fast, you are no longer in a position equal to the employer who has many applicants for the job. There is a third possibility. If you are an excellent match for the job and no other applicant comes close, you are at a significant advantage. A realistic attitude can avoid the first situation and good planning can usually avoid the second. In the third situation, you can destroy your advantage by becoming arrogant.

Be Yourself At Your Best

This book does not advocate putting on an act or trying to be someone else. Instead, we firmly believe there is an honest, successful approach to getting the right job offer:

- **Be Yourself:** Know yourself well. Find a match between your skills and professional goals on one hand and the employer's needs and professional rewards on the other. If the match is there and you present yourself well, you will maximize your chances for a successful interview. Trying to be someone else will undercut both your ability to present actual strengths and the interviewer's sense that you are being straight with him or her.

- **At your best:** You wouldn't go to a business meeting unprepared or with a bad attitude. You wouldn't go to work without combing your hair or brushing your teeth. Why? Because we need to be at our best in a professional context. How we behave when we are watching our favorite sporting event on a vacation day may be appropriate in that context, but not in a professional environment. Does that mean you should have a split personality or be unreal? No! It simply means that to succeed at an interview the professional in you, at your best, has to be presented.

Four Core Questions

Throughout this book, we give you dozens of examples of questions you may be asked. All of these could fit into one of the three core categories indicated below. These categories may help you organize your thinking and your answers:

1. **Why should we hire you?** Identify the skills, experiences and attitudes you possess which meet the firm's needs.

2. **Why do you want to work for us?** Your motivation is extremely important. Specify what it is about the job, the company and the industry which you find attractive.

3. **What do you know about my company?** Show that you did your research on the company in terms of its products, history, competition, challenges and financial situation.

4. **Do you have any questions for me?** If you want to be considered a serious candidate for the job, you must also ask questions at the interview. Good questions are a must. Chapter 7 examines how to do this.

Different Interview Formats

When we think of interviewing, we often envision two people in an office, the interviewer and the interviewee. For clarity of presentation this book is written with that scenario in mind. However, there are additional or alternative formats some employers use, so it pays to be prepared. In addition, our scenario is based on an **initial interview** (sometimes called a screening interview). The initial interview is your first round interview from which the prospective employer determines whether or not to invite you to a further round of interviews. However, the ideas and principles we present are also applicable for the follow-up or selection interviews to which only the best candidates from the initial interview are invited.

Interview Committee

You may be interviewed by a committee of two or more people. At first this may feel intimidating, but remember that you are facing potential colleagues, not a firing squad.

Each person on the committee will probably ask his/her own questions. That part is really not so different from a one-on-one interview. What's different is the etiquette of your response. As you begin your answer, speak directly to the individual who asked the question. Then, as you continue your response, establish brief eye contact with the other committee members. In this way you are including the whole group with the motion of your head and eyes.

The committee interview format could be to your advantage for several reasons.

- The firm has made a bigger investment in the interview process by devoting the time of more than one person to the interview.

- The committee members may be under less stress since each one can devote most of his/her time listening to your answers and taking notes rather than asking questions.

- There are more potential advocates for your candidacy.

Group Interview

You may be in a small group of job candidates who are interviewed together. Usually, a small committee will ask the questions. To succeed in this format, it is important to understand why it is used.

Many employers are interested in seeing how you will interact with peers. You could be the Albert Einstein of your profession and still not be an asset if your interpersonal relations are shaky, let alone contentious. This is particularly true where team work is central to getting things done.

The first key is this: participate, don't dominate. If the

first question is asked to the group as a whole (rather than to a specific individual) feel free to answer it. But give someone else the first crack at the **next** question.

The second key is: love thy neighbor. Think of the other candidates in the group as future colleagues, not competitors. Feel honored to be sharing the interview with such talented people.

If you want to disagree with someone in the group, do it in a positive way. You could say something like this:

"I think Hector made a good point, but I look at it differently..."

OR

"Marianne, I like what you said about the future importance of widgets to this industry. In that connection I want to add that gadgets may play a complementary role in any marketing program this firm develops..."

Remember to address your response initially to the interviewer who asked the question or the candidate whose idea you are discussing. Then bring the other members of the committee into the discussion with your eyes and head.

Lunch Interview

Sometimes you will be interviewed over a meal, let's say lunch. In principle, this is an interview with food on the table. If anything goes into your mouth make sure its your food, not your foot. In terms of food, order something which is easy to eat, moderately priced and familiar to your taste buds. The meal is still a business meeting. You don't want to spill spaghetti sauce on your clothes or to use the occasion for taste testing a new food.

Conversation may be casual, so be ready for some less than serious conversation topics. If there is some non-controversial, high profile topic which is of likely interest (let's say a national basketball championship) it pays to acquire at least a passing acquaintance with it.

The lunch interview format has some distinctive characteristics:

- Your interpersonal skills are all the more on display in this less structured environment.

- The lunch time format puts more flexible constraints on time and negates the potential distractions of the interviewer's work site.

- Since we were all taught not to chew with our mouth open, you have an extra incentive to pause before speaking.

But be careful:

- The "relaxed" environment of a fine restaurant may be a source of tension for some people. In that case go to lunch with a friend and practice interviewing over an easy to eat, moderately priced, familiar entree. Talk about some topics of mutual interest.

- Some people are so impressed by the restaurant they forget that every interaction is part of the interview process. Don't let your guard down. Similarly don't let the fine restaurant enter into your evaluation of the job if it is offered.

Telephone Interviews

To control expenses, some firms will conduct at least the initial (screening) interview over the phone. The firm's minimum goal is to eliminate the obviously inappropriate candidates. Your minimum goal is to be not obviously inappropriate. Here are some tips for acing the telephone interview.

- Prepare as you would for any other interview. The fact that the main characters are unable to see each other doesn't change the basic rules.

- Make sure you answer the phone at the arranged time in a clean, quiet place where you will not be interrupted.

- Form a mental image of a bright, friendly person on the other end of the phone.

- Have paper handy in case you want to take notes.

- Prepare some good questions to ask.

- Let your voice show enthusiasm.

- Be prepared for an interview ranging from a quick fifteen minutes to a more tiring hour.

- Have your resume handy in case you want to refer to it.

- Silence is not a bad sign. Don't stumble over yourself trying to end a silence at the other end of the phone.

Since your body language, so to speak, will be in your

voice, it is a good idea to get a bit pumped before the interview begins. It would be a self-destructive idea to think of this phone call as anything less than a business meeting that can have a major impact on your career.

Don't Be Caught Unaware

Imagine this scene. Ralph has sent out ten resumes and has followed up with phone calls a week later. So far, he has spoken to ten answering machines. No interviews, telephone or otherwise, have been arranged.

The phone rings. It's Denise Johansen from Maybeco calling. Denise would like to talk to Ralph about his resume. What should Ralph do?

The surprise telephone interview is a tool some firms use for two reasons. One is expense control, as we noted previously. A second is that the unexpected interview is thought to reveal the real you better.

Expect the unexpected. Here's what you can do.

1. Consider the call an unexpected pleasure, rather than an intrusion: "It's great to hear from you! I am very interested in your firm."

2. Have a brief log for each of the firms to which you applied. For each firm, have some quick notes about what they do and why you are interested in them. This information may already be available to you if you wrote a good cover letter with each resume.

Denise Johansen is probably going to ask you some basic questions about your motivation **for that job** and what you know **about Maybeco**. Based on your handy log, you can speak about the company's products, annual report, etc. and overcome the base line purpose of Denise's call:

To screen out candidates not worth pursuing.

An alternate approach is to say "Denise this is not a good moment to speak. Is there a time when I can get back to you?" The advantage of this approach is that you can buy some time to compose yourself if necessary. The disadvantage is that the loss of spontaneity means less credibility that this is the real you.

2

15 Ways to Ace Your Interview Before It Begins

Acing your interview starts long before the day it is scheduled. Your preparation determines your probability of success. This chapter will discuss the research and the attitudes you will need to succeed.

5 Strategic Steps

Ace #1: Your First Ace. Understand the Job

The purpose of the interview is to evaluate the match between you and the position which needs to be filled. Therefore, it makes good sense to understand the job as well as possible. Here are four ways to do that:

- **Written description:** Most job descriptions identify at least briefly the general goals to be achieved and the requisite attributes—skills, knowledge, abilities—of the ideal candidate. The interviewer will be evaluating the match between the job and you. Since the job description identifies the attributes you needed, you should be prepared to demonstrate that you possess them.

- **Oral description:** Once your interview is scheduled, you may be able to get an oral description of the job. A call to the human resource department may yield a person willing to discuss the job in greater detail. As with many aspects of interviewing, remember that the effort is nearly cost free, so you have nothing to lose by trying.

- **Similar job:** Try to speak with someone who has a similar job, even if it is with a different company. Reflections of a real live person add an important dimension to your understanding.

- **Generic sources:** There are several sources of generic job descriptions. Some you can access easily in the reference section of a good library. They are worth reading if you remember that any description which is broadly applicable will not be an exact picture of the particular position you are considering.

Occupational Outlook Handbook (OOH)

This reference produced by the federal Department of Labor gives several pages of descriptions for hundreds of job titles. These brief entries often include several paragraphs about skills you need in order to succeed in that field. Review the OOH for information you may not acquire from other sources.

Professional Associations

There are thousands of professional associations through-out the United States. Many of them publish inexpensive or free literature about careers in the field. If you are not already a member of an association related to the position you are considering, it is easy to access association names and addresses from Gale's ***Encyclopedia of Associations***.

Career Specific Books

If you are a recent college graduate or about to change fields, it is a good idea to read a book devoted specifically to the field you are trying to enter. One way to identify such books is to research **Books In Print** at your local library. The career or business section of a book store is also a good place to look.

Ace #2: Know the Prospective Employer

There are seven basic facts about your prospective employer you need to know before your interview. To your good fortune, this information is usually publicly available and easily accessible. Use this chart as a handy guide:

Basic Fact	Available Sources
1. Services, products	Annual report; promotional literature
2. Approximate measures; size	Annual report; news releases.
3. Profitability	Annual report; news releases.
4. History	Annual report; promotional literature
5. Self Definition	Annual report; promotional literature
6. Competition	Trade Press; specific books
7. Challenges	Annual report; business & general press; generic references, human

Here's how you can access the information you need:

- **World Wide Web:** Many firms have a home page in the World Wide Web. These can be excellent sources of information regarding all seven basic facts in this ace.

- **Annual Report:** Any company that is publicly owned (i.e. issues share of stock available for purchase by the public) must issue an annual report. These are often available in libraries and should be sent to you upon request by the firm.

- **Promotional Literature:** Every business sells some service or product. In most cases the firm produces some form of promotional literature to attract potential customers and clients. This is true of small firms as well as large. Promotional literature should be yours for the asking.

- **News Releases:** Keeping current with the general and business press is a good idea under any circumstances. Knowledge helps you do your job better. To check recent news stories utilize Infotract, available in many libraries.

- **Trade Press:** Most professions have at least one trade journal. These are excellent tools for keeping current with issues important to the field. Reading them will also help you think and talk more like an insider.

- **Reference Texts:** Some texts, available in libraries, are useful and provide relatively quick read. *Hoover's 500* gives short company profiles for 500 firms and identifies the described firm's competitors. *U.S. Industry Surveys* discusses the state of the industry and the main players in it.

- **Human Insights:** Employees, competitors, suppliers, and clients of your prospective employer are all good sources of information. Some books which will help you access these people for informational interviews are noted in Chapter 6.

Ace #3: Anticipate the Company's Agenda

You can strengthen your hand by anticipating what the company will try to learn about you at the interview. Why is your interview being held at all? From the company's point of view, they have a business need, and they believe that you may be a good candidate to serve that need. Your best clues are understanding the job and the company. I suggest making a list of what the company needs on the left side of a piece of paper, then proceed to your next ace.

Ace #4: Prepare Your Own Agenda

Match the list you constructed anticipating the company's agenda with **specific examples** of how you have demonstrated, achieved or learned those attributes in the past. Your combined list might look something like the table on page 19. This chart reflects a candidate who is **not an obvious choice** but is preparing to show that s/he is at least a **plausible** choice.

Ace #5: Dispel Interview Myths

Many people go through the interview process bearing the burden of interview myths. Dispelling those myths will make your interview process less nerve-racking and more successful.

The employer needs (This chart uses market research as an example).	Examples to show that I offer what the employer needs.
Analysis Skills	Analyzed data regarding returns while at Consumerco.
Research Skills	Researched potential suppliers in terms of location, quality and price while at Sourceco.
Presentation Skills	Presented numerous class projects while in college; made presentations in fraternities/sororities while promoting Spring Vacation Packages Associates.
Writing Skills	Wrote articles for College Press; wrote recommendations to minimize flow of returns while at Consumerco.

- **The Driver's Seat Myth**—Contrary to myth, the employer is not in the driver's seat. In fact, no one is. You want/need a new job, the firm wants/needs a new employee. Just as the firm can interview many candidates, you can interview with many potential employers. Nevertheless, remember to be courteous to everyone and avoid any arrogance on your part.

- **The Magic Words Myth**—Some people go into the interview trying to say what the interviewer wants to hear. But there are no predefined, engraved in platinum phrases that will get you the job offer. To the extent that the interviewer has a mind set about what s/he wants to hear, it is this: Demonstrate that you can do the job.

- **Dress and Success**—Although it is important to dress for your interview, the most you can usually achieve is to make dress a neutral factor. That is, don't dress inappropriately. By wearing standard, sensible business clothing, having shined shoes and a reasonable hair style you will avoid the inappropriate. If you are still nervous about dress, lean towards being more rather than less conservative. This is especially true of initial interviews. After you have met some people in the firm, you have a reasonable basis for modifying your dress if you wish.

Attitudes to Ace Your Interviews (10 more Aces)

Having the proper attitude is critical to interview success. What you are feeling on the inside will affect what you do, what you say and what impressions you convey subjectively to your interviewer.

Ace #6: Be Courteous to Everyone

Courtesy is in order as a matter of general principle. This includes your approach to receptionists and other people you meet who don't seem to be decision makers. **Anyone** you meet may be asked to express an opinion about you.

Ace #7: Let Your Enthusiasm Show

Enthusiasm for the job is a positive characteristic. Wouldn't you rather be near someone who is enthusiastic than someone who is reluctant or who lacks a spark? Suppressing enthusiasm is counter-productive. Playing hard to get is a losing game. Of course, you don't want to be **so** enthusiastic that you jump out of your seat while responding to questions.

Ace #8: Respect the Other Applicants

Think of the other applicants as marvelous, talented people with whom you would love to work. From the employer's perspective, how you relate to other applicants may indicate how you would relate to your co-workers. Respect is obviously a winner. In addition there's nothing you can do to stop the other applicants from competing with you anyway. In America, we don't shoot the competition.

Ace #9: Put Your Energy Into Things You Can Influence

Energy, whether physical or mental, is limited. Put your energy into things that can influence the outcome of your interview. Examples would be research and preparing your questions for the interviewer. Don't waste your energy worrying about things you can't influence like how many other applicants there are.

Ace #10: Be Yourself at Your Best

Your job at the interview is to be yourself at your best. Putting that into perspective, you are neither an obvious choice who will be offered the job for sure nor a hopeless incompetent who would be lucky to get his/her next job.

Ace #11: Respect the Interviewer's Intelligence, Prerogatives and Space

Some people go into an interview needlessly combative and overly assertive. While the cause may be sheer anxiety, these are not constructive attitudes. Here are some helpful thoughts.

- **Respect the Interviewer's Intelligence**—Your interviewer probably is intelligent in general, although
  ignorant about you in particular. Assuming your
  interviewer is unintelligent will not help you convey a
  favorable impression, so it is a useless attitude in any
  event. Keep in mind that intelligence is a common
  attribute among human resource professionals as
  well as line managers.

- **Respect the Interviewer's Prerogatives**—Setting the
  tone of the interview is the interviewer's prerogative.
  Perhaps there are policy or practical reasons for
  being formal or informal. Perhaps it is his or her
  personal preference. Either way, let it be.

- **Respect the Interviewer's Space**—In a sense, you are
  in his/her working home. Some people will take
  understandable offense if you put objects on their
  desk or take other liberties like rearranging the
  furniture. Give the interviewer a chance to invite you
  to sit down by words or gestures. If you don't get the
  invitation, sit down anyway.

Ace #12: Be Positive

It is better to think of things in the positive because you will
then express yourself in a more positive tone. For example,
it is better to think about reasons for wanting a new job
rather than dwelling on reasons for leaving your current
one. It is better to state a preference than a dislike (Would
you prefer a house guest who says "I don't like coffee" or
one who says "I prefer tea")? Positive thinking leads to
positive statements which lead to conveying positive
impressions. Negative thinking tends to have the opposite
effect.

Doing it Badly

Some people show **disrespect** for the interviewer and torpedo their chances. Here are some examples interviewers shared with me.

■ **Respect the layman:** The interviewer is intelligent, although s/he may be relatively uninformed in your field of expertise. Tailor your remarks as you would when explaining a technical point to any layman you would deal with professionally, such as customer, a supplier, a co-worker with another function. Talking over their heads will create a negative feeling towards you. So will talking down, not to mention refusing to discuss the subject because "the interviewer wouldn't understand." Your goal is to win the job offer, not to show how smart you are.

■ **The Age Issue:** Sometimes you may be interviewed by a person who is younger than you. Statements like "My kids are older than you" or "My, you seem young" give the impression that you don't take the other person seriously. Young or old, that person will have a voice in determining who gets the job offer.

Here are some other examples:

Negative Approach	Positive Approach
I hated sitting in the office all day.	I preferred going out to meet clients.
That's wrong.	A better or another way would be...
I didn't like (what ever) so I decided to do (something else).	I decided to do this because...
I am not good with computer stuff like e-mail.	For me, traditional communication, like the telephone, has worked very well.
No, unless...	Yes, if...

Ace #13: Be Principled, but Flexible

Yes, there are standards of conduct you can insist on in any job you would take. These may be reflected in clients. On the other hand, be flexible. Stand by your standards if they are a matter of immutable principle. Be flexible if they are a matter of preference.

Here are some examples:

Principles	Preferences
Honesty	Bluntness; circumspection
Doing a good job	Workaholic; balanced life
Timeliness	Immediately; before deadline
Courtesy	Formality; informality
Protecting proprietary information	Discussing or not discussing awkward subjects.

Ace #14: Put the Interview Into Perspective

What's the worst thing that can happen? You won't get this particular job. You will still be alive and able to interview for another job another day. Realizing that should help alleviate some anxiety. Besides it may be that by not offering you the job the employer has saved you from a career mistake you didn't foresee.

My own career provides an example. I took what was supposed to be a one-year assignment in a college career placement office while I was completing an MBA at night. A prominent firm interviewed me for a position in economic and financial analysis. The interviewer said to me, "Richard I know you could do this job, but I am not going to offer it to you." The first half of the sentence made me ecstatic; the second half brought me down with a crash. But then the interviewer explained with an observation for which I remain grateful, sixteen years later. She said "You gave all the right answers, but I looked at your face. You were much more enthused discussing career placement than return-on-investment."

than return-on-investment."

She was right. By not offering me the job, the interviewer helped me stay on a career path which has made me both happy and successful.

Ace #15: Know What the World Owes You

The world does not owe you anything. No one is obligated to offer you a job any more than you are obligated to accept a job that is offered. Your difficult family circumstances or your years of selfless service to another employer don't create any obligations for a prospective employer. Leave those thoughts at home.

Where Are We Now?

In this chapter we looked at fifteen ways to ace your interview before it even begins. First there were five strategic steps of preparation. Then we looked at ten attitudes to ace your interview.

In the next chapter, we will look at fifteen dynamite principles for giving good answers.

3

15 Dynamite Principles for Giving Good Answers

Ace #16: Ace the Small Talk

Small talk is no small matter. As at most business meetings, your interview will probably start with small talk for three reasons. First, the interviewer wants to break the ice with you. One way is to start a discussion about something you won't find threatening. Second, the interviewer wants to make you less nervous. Meetings are more productive if the participants are somewhat relaxed. Third, your interviewer may want to hear how you present yourself when discussing an apparently mundane topic. This is a useful tool both with external clients and other employees. In some cases, if you can't make small talk, you can't get the job.

The key is to listen to the interviewer's remark and respond in an upbeat vein. For example, if the interviewer says "That blizzard is really raising havoc out there," you can follow with a remark like, "It certainly is. I am glad we were both able to make it in today despite the storm." Avoid a negative or self-centered response like, "It sure is, I got soaked just getting here." Also avoid a non-communicative response like a simple "Yes."

Many people learn how to "small talk" through the development of their social life. In a sense, it comes naturally. For others, small talk with strangers may feel uncomfortable. That's O.K. You can practice small talk.

I can testify to that fact from my own experience. I started in the career development profession in 1980. At that point, based on both my undergraduate liberal arts degree and my MBA studies, I could discuss business theory, the state of the world, theology, nuclear arms control and a host of heavy subjects. But I couldn't make small talk. This concerned me since it was a professional impediment and wasn't helping with my social life either. I read a book which described some basic skills in making conversation. I summarized what I learned and have used it as a guiding principle for making both small talk and general conversation ever since:

- Listen to the statement the other person makes.

- Follow up on the same theme. (Example: The weather certainly is beautiful. Have you had a chance to be outside much this week? I don't follow the football team very closely, but I know they're doing really well this year. Are you a sports fan?)

Small talk is not wasted time. It's an opportunity for you to get comfortable in the interview room and to practice listening to what your interviewer has to say. In that sense, it's like an athlete warming up before the start of a game. Even if what s/he does on the sideline doesn't show up in the final score, the warm-up is essential to success in the game.

Doing it Badly

It's possible to shoot yourself in the foot with small talk. Interviewer: "Ralph, I'm glad you could make it in today despite the blizzard."

Ralph: "I had a general sense of how to get here, but I got lost. Luckily, your office is closer than I thought or I would have been late."

Ralph has hurt himself in two and possibly three ways:

- He didn't have enough sense to check on directions.
- His being on time seems to be a matter of luck.
- Ralph forgot to show interest in the interviewer, perhaps by asking if s/he had a hard time traveling in the blizzard.

Ace #17: Ace the Opening Questions

After a few minutes of small talk, your interviewer will ask a question which is more related to the heart of your interview. Typical opening questions might be:

- "Bill, why do you want to leave your current employer?"
- "Leslie, please tell me about yourself."
- "Alice, tell me why you chose to become an engineer."

Your answer to this first question is especially important for two reasons. First the interviewer is likely to ask one or two **follow-up** questions based on your answer. Therefore you should include in your response topics **you would like to discuss further.** In this way, you can set the agenda for your interview, at least partially. Second, during the first five minutes, the interviewer usually forms an impression of you, positive or negative. The rest of the interview serves to confirm or reverse that initial impression. The interviewer will tend to hear what confirms his/her initial impression and to screen out information which conflicts with it. This does **not** mean that the interview is over in five minutes. It does mean that the early minutes of an interview are especially important.

To ace the first question include at least one positive attribute about yourself about which the prospective employer could ask more in a follow-up question. For example:

- **Bill** (leaving current employer): "I have had a good experience with my current employer and I am proud of my accomplishments. For example, I developed a loyal staff which is moving up in the firm. We reduced overhead by 20%, opened some new markets and established better ties with existing clients.

    "At this point in my life, I want to take on some fresh challenges. That's what attracted me to Yourco."

- **Leslie** (describing herself): "People who have seen me work would describe me as a thorough manager who produces an excellent product, on time and under pressure. I do this by combining my talents in research and analysis with my interpersonal skills and communication ability. I want to add that I have an excellent staff. Without all of us working together, we couldn't achieve the same results." (**Hint:** Leslie utilized the table she made in preparing her own agenda. Ace 4)

- **Alice** (responding to a question about career choice): "I chose to become an engineer for several reasons. One is that I excelled in mathematics and the natural sciences. In addition I enjoyed reading engineering magazines before I even entered college. Once I entered the engineering program, the group projects we worked on in class were exciting. In fact in my favorite project, we made some interesting observations about the impact of gravity on small bridges. That's one of the reasons I am excited to be interviewing with Build-A-Bridge, Inc."

Ace #18: Know How to Listen

An important part of communication is knowing how to listen. Only by listening carefully to the question is it possible to give a responsive answer. In particular, listen to the **intent** of the question. What is it that the interviewer really wants to know?

For example, let's look again at Leslie's example in Ace #17. Leslie thought about the intent of "tell me about yourself" and realized that the interviewer was referring to job related aspects of Leslie, particularly those which could be reasons to offer her a job. A discussion of Leslie's family, hobbies, golf handicap would address the literal sense of the question, but not its intent.

Know how many parts there are to the question. It is not unusual to be asked a two or three part question. In response you could start by saying "There seem to be three parts to that question. Let me address each of them," or "As I understand it, both parts of your question are really related..."

If you are not sure about the intent of the question, ask. You could say "I want to make sure I understand your question properly. Are you interested in knowing more about my writing skills?" Remember our general principle that an interview is a business meeting between equals. At a business meeting, you would clarify a question if necessary before giving your response.

Ace #19: The Productive Pause

No one expects you to respond to a question in real time as though you were a computer. Part of your value to the employer is your ability to give a considered reply before giving an answer. So take a moment to collect your thoughts before responding. Objectively, your response is likely to be better. Subjectively you are more likely to convey the impression of a person who thinks before s/he speaks. That is a valuable trait. If a particular question needs some extra thought you could say, "That's an interesting question. Let me think about that for a moment."

Your pause is helpful to the interviewer as well. It gives him/her a chance to switch from speaking mode to listening mode. Since interviews are difficult for the interviewer as well, this is not a small point.

There are two other good reasons to pause. First, pausing induces you to wait until the other person is finished speaking. That will help you avoid annoying the interviewer by interrupting. Second, if you pause to reflect, you are more likely to convey sincerity and less likely to appear pre-programmed.

Ace #20: A Positive Characteristic

Each question presents an opportunity to tell the interviewer at least one good thing about you that indicates you would be a good employee. Remember Ace 4, preparing your own agenda. Know what points you want to make about yourself and include at least one with every response. For example:

> Q. "Hanna, what do you think the greatest challenge to our industry will be over the next five years?"

Here is a chance for Hanna to show at least two good things about herself: that she has thought about this issue; that she offers something to meet future challenges.

> A. "A growing challenge to firms in this industry is

being big enough to have clout with suppliers while being agile enough to respond quickly to customers. I had to struggle with a challenge like that at Formerco. Would you like to hear about how that experience would be helpful to Yourco?"

Doing it Badly

Imagine what would happen if Hanna had responded "I haven't thought much about future challenges because my involvement is with day to day issues. If I get the job, I will add that to my list of concerns." Hanna would have failed to show any prior thought to a vital subject, and that's bad enough. She also would have seemed to view challenges as something to put in a to-do list rather than as a mega-issue directly affecting the firm's future.

Ace #21: Give Examples

Your responses will be much more credible if you support them with examples. Which of the following responses would be more helpful to the job applicant?

Q. "Why do you feel you would make a good sales representative, Peter?"

A. "I have good time management and persuasion skills."

Or

A. "I have good time management, persuasion and listening skills. Let me give you some examples. On my current job, I make 20% more sales calls than the office average, even though I have a larger territory to cover. I have persuaded customers to give our product a try even when they already felt overstocked with a competitor's product. Many of my customers have commented that they like doing business with me because I listen to their needs instead of just pushing my own agenda."

Doing It Badly

Here are some poor ways to convey a positive characteristic about yourself.

- I know everything there is to know about this job.
  (Hint: Nobody does; if it were true you would have no room for growth.)
- Nobody else could do the job as well as I can.
  (Hint: You can't be a judge of other people's talent.)
- I am a friend of _____
  (Hint: Name dropping implies negatives like loyalty to someone else or insecurity in your own talent).
- I belong to _____ ethnic group.
- I can be whatever you need me to be; what are you looking for?

Ace #22: Give Results; Quantify If Possible

Identifying **results** that you achieved is another way to add power and credibility to your interview answers. After all, you are paid to produce results not just exert effort. Your answer will be even stronger if you can **quantify** the results you achieved. For example:

Q. "Dan, what achievements are you most proud of when you think back over the last few years?"

A. "I was hired to achieve three main objectives, and I exceeded them in less time than anyone imagined. Let me be specific. I increased market share by 23%, introduced three new products within 2 years and cut response time to clients from two days to less than one."

A good interviewer may follow up with a "how" question:

Q. "Dan, how did you increase market share by 23%?" That of course is fine with you because it offers an opportunity to present more positive characteristics of importance to your potential next employer.

Compare the answer Dan gave above to a response which is not quantified.

A. "I achieved three main goals: increasing market share, introducing new products and cutting response time."

This response would not be awful, but it would be less powerful and credible than the answer Dan actually gave.

Ace #23: Display Your Research

One of the critical components of interview success is doing your pre-interview research (See Ace 1 and 2). The related principle is to **display** your research in some of your answers. For example:

Q. "Jennifer, why do you want to work for this company?"

A. "I researched your firm and found some very attractive facts. The first is that you have been consistently profitable, even when the industry as a whole had off years. Second **Women's Weekly** magazine rated this firm highly in terms of providing women with an equal chance to advance. Third, the **Gadget Gazette** described your new products as proof that this firm provides capital resources to support promising ideas."

Doing it Badly

Compare the good answer Jennifer actually gave with a response which doesn't display her research:

A. "Your firm has been profitable even when others in the industry have not. Second, women can get ahead here. Third, I understand that this firm provides capital resources to support promising ideas."

Although the above response is not terrible, it missed the chance to impress the interviewer with the degree of Jennifer's research.

Ace #24: Keep It Focused

Staying focused on the question at hand is an important communication skill. It may help you to stay focused if you keep your answer to between six and eight sentences in length. That is long enough to present one or more positive characteristics that match the employer's needs. At the same time, it is concise enough not to exhaust the interviewer's desire to listen.

There is no need to burden yourself wondering whether you should be saying more. You may simply ask the interviewer, "Would you like me to tell you more about that?" or "Have I answered your question?"

The six-to-eight sentence answer is not a hard and fixed rule. It is a guideline to help you avoid overly short answers which provide no information, or longer answers which ramble. If you give a focused answer, its length is not critical. In multi-part questions, use the "six-to-eight" guideline for each part. Similarly, if you are giving examples, use the "six-to-eight" guideline for each example.

Ace #25: Have Problem Solving Ideas

One of the best attributes you can bring to an employer is your problem solving capability. The need for problem solvers is generic to all professions. It is always possible that an interviewer will ask you directly about this by saying "Describe a recent problem you have experienced at work and how you solved it." However, there is no need to depend on that eventuality. Instead, you can introduce a problem solving example like this:

Q. "You mention inventory management on your resume as a major responsibility at your current company. We don't have any inventory here. Is your experience really related to our needs?"

A. "One of the things I showed through inventory management is my ability to solve major problems and anticipate new ones before they hurt us. Let me give an example for each case. A major problem is carrying cost. I assigned workers to a small third shift to expedite shipments during busy seasons. This reduced our carrying cost by one-third while making our end-user clients happier.

"I also short-stopped a potential problem. As we started to carry higher value products, the potential for 'shrinkage' became more serious. I researched anti-theft procedures and devices, in part by consulting with our insurance carrier. As a result, I put in place a system which reduced shrinkage to zero.

"The same thought process I used at Formerco might help relieve the turn-around time problem many firms in this industry are experiencing."

Words Have Meaning

Ace #26: Avoid Using Words Loosely

Imagine a situation like this. Dahlia answers a question, let's say one about her job expectations, and says: "I am looking for a challenging job that will keep me busy. By proving my contributions to the firm, I want to become successful."

Let's hope that Dahlia didn't use words like "challenging" and "successful" simply because they sound good. It would be perfectly reasonable for the interviewer to follow up by asking "What about this job would you find challenging?" or "What does success mean to you?" If Dahlia has a clear, reasonable perception of "challenging" and "successful" she will be ready to give a good answer. If not, you can almost hear the hot air going out of Dahlia's interview balloon.

Ace #27: Language in Common Usage

An underlying theme in this book is that a job interview is a business meeting between equals. At a business meeting, clear communication is critical. In that connection, use words in the way that they are commonly understood. Using your own private language only raises barriers to your getting hired.

Unfortunately private language hurt Herman at his interview for a job he could have won and done. Herman said something like this: "One of the things I really like about accounting is that it is so creative."

The interviewer had seldom heard accounting and creative linked together before. When they **had** been linked it implied a certain ethical laxness. The interviewer and Herman got enmeshed in trying to understand what Herman meant. Finally, Herman thought it through more clearly and said, "I suppose I mean that accounting requires thinking, not just crunching numbers. That's what creative means to me."

Understandably, the interviewer's mind began to question Herman's communication skills, an avoidable consequence which hurt Herman's job prospects.

Ace #28: Buzz Words: Industry v. Firm Specific

In the previous two aces we discussed knowing what you mean by the words you use and using words as they are generally understood. What about that special lexicon called "buzz words?" These are terms which have a specific currency in a particular profession. I suggest a few guidelines:

- Don't use them just to show that you have heard the term. Otherwise, you are likely to sound like a name dropper at a cocktail party.

- If you use a buzz word, make sure you know what it means in the context of the industry or profession for which you are interviewing.

- Use a generic, standard English term instead of a buzz word which was common at a previous job but may not be immediately understood in another place.

- If the interviewer uses a buzz word, make sure you know what s/he means before answering the question

Your Worst Nightmare

Over the years, I have asked thousands of people what their worst fear at an interview would be. Here are the two most common nightmares and how to deal with them.

Ace #29: Going Blank

Many people express fear about going blank at an interview. This is a relatively rare occurrence. If it does happen to you, turn the situation to your advantage: "John, you know I am so enthusiastic about this job that I am really nervous. My mind has just gone blank on your question. Would you mind repeating it? (or . . . Could we come back to it later?)"

Ace #30: Dealing With Clueless

Being clueless is no fun, but it's not necessarily a catastrophe either. An interviewer is hardly likely to ask you a question you would have no reason to know about. Similarly, if you've done your preparation, you should be at least conversant, if not expert, on any subject likely to come up. However, if you are asked a question and you are truly clueless, don't try to fudge. You could say: "Honestly, I just don't know very much at all about that. My responsibilities have been in a different area. Would you please clarify why you are asking?"

The response to the last sentence may clarify the question and return the interview to a path you are more comfortable treading upon.

Clueless has a cousin. "I'll say something stupid." It's unlikely that any one statement will sink your chances. In terms of embarrassment, only you and the interviewer are going to know what you said. It won't appear as a headline in your hometown newspaper or be a subject of gossip at your favorite watering hole.

Where Are We Now?

In this chapter, we looked at fifteen dynamite principles for giving good answers. These included acing the small talk and the first question, giving examples, displaying your research and using words well. In the next chapter, we will look at ten strategies to ace potential or expressed interviewer objections.

4

10 Strategies to Ace Objections

The prospective employer picked you for an interview because s/he saw a potential match between the firm's needs and you based on your resume. Still, there may be some "objections" in the interviewer's mind. Objections are doubts or "yes-but" factors that need to be addressed and laid to rest. This chapter will show you common objections to anticipate and how to address them.

Ace #31: Too Little/Too Much Experience

The interviewer may have in mind a certain number of years of experience that the ideal candidate should have. Since your resume earned you the interview, you know that your experience level hasn't stood in your way at this stage. Still, the interviewer's concerns must be addressed.

- **Too Little:** What the employer really needs is a talent level. The length of time they have in mind reflects an estimation of how long they think it would take to

develop the needed level of talent. Your task is to
identify the talent you have, how you developed it,
and how that talent addresses the job's requirements, irrespective of the particular time frame
involved.

Q. Celia, you've been in your current job for about
three years. Do you think that has prepared you
for the kind of job we are discussing today?

A. Yes, I do. As my manager has said, I have ac-
complished in three years what most people
would achieve in five or six. I am dedicated to my
work and, frankly, I have been blessed with the
right tools. In addition, I have had the opportunity to work in a variety of situations in those
three years. I can give you some examples if you
would like.

Before responding, Celia could ask "Are you concerned
that the number of years I have spent in my current position would be a problem for Yourco?" That might clarify the
interviewer's concern.

- **Too much:** As a general principle, the terms "over-
qualified" or "under qualified" are misnomers. The
real concern is that you may not be a good match.
Too much experience may really mean the candidate has stagnated, s/he is set in their ways, their
salary and status expectations will be unrealistic for
that firm or the job will not be a challenge. Even if
the candidate was simply very happy with what s/he
has been doing, this is still a point the interviewer
may want to probe. Here's what to do:

Q. Dan, you have been a manager in consumer soft

goods for ten years now. That's a long time in one job, isn't it?

If you have reason to think the objection is that you have stagnated, you could show that in fact you have continued growing.

A. One of the things I like about my job is that it has changed enormously, and I have continuously grown with it. Ten years ago, I managed $40 million of men's underwear. Today, I manage $250 million, including every aspect from choosing manufacturers and negotiating contracts to consumer research and advertising. I have the same title but in substance the job has grown tremendously. One of the things I have demonstrated over these last ten years is a great deal of adaptability.

If you have reason to believe that the concern is that your expectations are unrealistic, frame the answer a bit differently by changing the way you end your response.

A. "..I have shown that I can grow with new responsibilities and adapt to new challenges. I realize of course that Yourco is in a different industry from my current employer, so I can't just pick-up straight from where I would be leaving-off."

Dan could ask "Are you concerned that I might have stagnated?" or, "Are you concerned that my expectations may be unrealistic?" before beginning his response to the question if he feels comfortable in doing so.

Ace #32: Experience is in a Different Industry/Career Change

Your objective is to show two things. First, that you understand the industry of your potential employer. That can come from your research (see Ace #2). Second, you need to demonstrate that the skills and attributes your next employer needs are those you have demonstrated in your current job or other fairly recent experience. Third, your experience in another industry may in itself be an advantage for a new employer. (see Aces #3 and #4).

For example:

Q. Harry, your experience has been in the stratospheric balloon industry. We're in deep-sea submersibles. That's a different kettle of fish, isn't it?

A. "I've given a good deal of thought to that issue. From my viewpoint as a manufacturing professional, the two industries have a lot in common. Both are highly technical products with a limited number of users. Both come with high price tags and need to pass through a competitive bid process. Both require careful attention to the needs of the end-user at every stage of development. Both require co-operative relationships among the engineers, the business professionals and the people on the shop floor. Those are all areas where my current expertise could be transferred to your firm. In addition, my experience with another industry gives me the advantage of having some measure of an outside perspective."

Ace #33: Job Loss/Resume Gaps

The good news about job loss is this: Because it is so common today, it no longer carries the stigma it once did. The underlying concern at your interview is that your job loss may have been the result of malfeasance or poor performance. It is important to address questions about job loss honestly and forthrightly:

> Q. "Arnie, you are no longer working at Formerco. Was your separation voluntary?"

> A. "No, it wasn't. I really loved working at Former-co. Unfortunately, my function was eliminated in a downsizing."

Or

> A. "No, it wasn't. I was a strong advocate for a policy which was ultimately rejected by senior management. That hurt me when my department was reorganized. One thing I learned from that experience is to involve more people up front before pushing my personal policy preferences."

In this response Arnie is doing three things. First, he is being brief, a good approach under the circumstances. Second, he is being forthright in his answer. That's a positive statement about his character. Third, Arnie shows that he has learned from his mistake. That makes it less likely that he will repeat that mistake on his next job. Arnie should be prepared if the interviewer follows-up with a question about the particular policies Arnie alluded to.

A similar situation exists for an individual who has gaps on their resume, perhaps a woman who is returning to the work force after a period at home. The underlying concerns which must be addressed are: Does she really want the job or does she just want to get out of the house? Will she have difficulty relating to people who are younger but have a higher position? Is she out-of-touch with current issues and methods of operation?

> Q. Alise, as you know our industry has changed since your last full time job ten years ago. How would you compare the industry now to the way it was then?

It is important not to allow these doubts to linger. You could say something like the following.

Before answering, Alise pauses. She realizes that her absence from the work world is a potential barrier to her re-entry. Rather than merely giving an erudite rendition of "compare and contrast," she seizes the opportunity to alleviate a doubt about herself.

> A. "Things certainly have changed in the last ten years and I don't want to pretend that I am at the same level of professional expertise as a person who has been working straight through.
>
> "I have been following the industry closely, especially over the past year or so. I read the trade journals and have lunch with people in the field at least twice a month. We have a home computer. I took some training to become adept at using it for research and communication. I worked hard to establish a career in this field before I started my family, and I want to re-establish my career now that my children are in school. I realize that my manager may be younger than I am, but that comes with the territory."

Ace #34: Adjustment to the Firm's Culture

Every place of work has its own way of doing things and its own operating philosophy. Sometimes this is referred to as the firm's culture. Even a talented person's effectiveness would be limited if s/he were unable to adjust to a new culture. Perhaps your current firm is highly structured and stable and the potential employer is entrepreneurial and changing. Or it may be that you want to change from a stereotypical nine-to-five environment to one where ambition drives a longer day. Allay doubts by saying something like this:

Q. "Rose, you have been working in a forty-hour week environment for a number of years. Sounds like a good work life to me. Why would you want to leave it?"

A. "My current employer is fair and has provided a pleasant place to work. However, I am looking for a work environment where an ambitious person can get ahead if she works hard and produces excellent results.

Rose is wise in two ways. First, she shows the ambition and results-orientation needed in her prospective new job. Second, she does not badmouth anybody in her current job.

Ace #35: Missing a Specific Skill or Attribute

Nobody is perfect and you shouldn't pretend to be. On the other hand, you do want to remove doubts about your match with the needs of the job. For the case of a missing skill or attribute, there are two approaches you can take: compensating skill or corrective steps.

Let's look at an example that utilizes both approaches:

Q. "Howard, is there anything about this job that you would find difficult?"

A. "That's a good question. A few moments ago we discussed some of the skills and attributes I can bring to this job. Another attribute is realism. I realize that I don't have the degree of supervisory experience or technical knowledge the ideal candidate you described would have. However, I have shown my ability to get things done as chair of the local Bear Benevolent Society. I am coming up to speed on technical issues by reading the trade press and I will be taking a good evening course at the local college's continuing education program."

Ace #36: Is the Objection a Fact or Misperception?

Make a basic distinction, at least in your own mind: Is the objection based on fact or is it a misperception? If it is a fact, attempt to minimize its significance or identify a skill or attribute which offsets the one that is lacking. On the other hand, if the objection is based on a misperception, clarify this for the interviewer.

Q. "David, you have been working in public service. Our company is organized for profit. How would you adjust to such a different environment?"

A. "I think I know what you mean. Many people don't realize that in public service we have to be conscious of cost, quality of service and the satisfaction of our clients. Business is answerable to demanding stockholders; we're answerable to a demanding legislature. If the service you provide your clients is not excellent, you will lose revenue. If the service we provide is not excellent, we will lose funding.

"The need to deliver excellent service at a controlled cost is common to us both. The difference is that if I make a profit, I could be arrested."

David responded intelligently here. Rather than contradicting the interviewer, David indicated that **many** people share a misperception. David proceeded to show the commonality between public service and for-profit environments. He skirted the issue of differences (e.g. civil service protection) but added a note of socially acceptable humor.

Ace #37: Address, Don't Argue

The point of your interview is to win the job offer, not to score debating points. When you address an objection, do so in a professional manner by presenting the applicable facts. Don't take the objection personally or start an argument.

Q. "Jeanne, your experience is in small organizations, one of which went belly-up. How would you make it in a large organization like ours?"

A. "The common element in both environments is to establish good relationships so you can get things done. Many of the functions which are done in-house here were done by outside vendors at my previous job. I was able to get good products at a good price, in part because I know how to work with people. The difference I see here is that there is a more established structure. I believe that won't be a hard adjustment to make.

"By the way, the firm that went belly-up praised my services while I was there. Unfortunately it was undercapitalized."

Stating the same facts in the wrong way, you could shoot yourself in the foot:

Doing It Badly

Argumentative Answer: "I don't see how you can say that! Working in a small firm is no bed of roses. There are endless outside vendors to deal with and each has their own agenda. A little structure wouldn't be a bad thing from my point of view. Besides, big doesn't scare me."

It is important to put a stated objection in the proper perspective. It is serious and must be allayed. On the other hand, the objection is probably not intended to be hostile or offensive. Understanding that will help you respond in a constructive way:

A. "You may be concerned about my willingness and ability to work late when necessary. Let me assure you that I have made adequate childcare arrangements. There won't be any logistic problems or mental distractions on that score."

Doing It Badly

If you take the question as hostile or offensive, the tone of your response is liable to change for the worse:

"Yes, I have children. It's possible for a woman to be a good mother and still do a good job, you know. Maybe you didn't have to learn that balancing act, but I have proven myself good at it."

Ace #38: Discover Unspoken Objections

Sometimes you will notice a quizzical look on an interviewer's face or some uncomfortable body language. Rather than wonder "Have I done something wrong?" ask. You could say "Would you like me to clarify anything I have said" or "Is there anything I have said which has left any doubts in your mind about me?"

Toward the end of your interview you could say, "I want to make sure that I have addressed everything you wanted to know about my skills and attributes. Are there any areas of doubt or concern that we should explore a bit further?"

You may even want to be more specific if you sense that the interviewer has particular doubts that s/he hasn't expressed. For example, the interviewer may have given you a complete job description and asked "Is there any reason you would not be able to perform these duties perhaps with some reasonable accommodation on our part?" Assume that you said "no" but feel that the interviewer is still uncertain. You could add:

"You may be wondering about this wheelchair. My condition is the result of an auto accident. I'm not carrying some sort of contagious disease. My attendance record speaks for itself. By the way, I can drive my own car when travel is required."

If you sense that there may be some concern about

your age, you could say: "I don't want to leave any doubts about my readiness to report to someone younger. Actually, it wouldn't be anything new. I volunteer as an assistant coach for high-school age kids and the head coach is in his thirties. The president of my Community Action Council is thirty-five, and I serve on her executive board."

Ace #39: Raise Potential Objection Yourself

In Chapter 2, we discussed anticipating the company's agenda and preparing your own. Comparing these two agendas, you may sense that there are some potential weaknesses in your candidacy. There are several ways to initiate a discussion about them:

- Ask a broad question like this one: "Are there any questions about my experiences or skills that you would want me to discuss in greater detail? I want to clarify any doubts that may be in your mind."

- Ask about a specific doubt: "Are you in any way concerned about my level of computer skills?"

- Offer a compensatory example. "You mentioned earlier how important team work is to Thisco. I realize that most of my professional experience hasn't been in organized teams, so I would like to tell you about my success in the community team which sponsored a Love Our Town business promotion campaign."

Ace #40: Be Prepared for Improper Objections

Some potential objections may be subject to legal considerations. These can be anticipated, so you should plan
what to do in these situations before your interview begins.

As a general rule of thumb, an employer has the right
to ask about your ability to do the job, but may be forbidden to ask about some potential barriers.

- **Disability:** If you can do the job, a physical or
  mental disability shouldn't stand in your way. It
  is forbidden to ask "do you have such and such
  a disability." However, you could be asked, "Is
  there anything that would prevent you from lifting
  boxes?" or "...that would prevent you from traveling to sales calls?" if those activities are essential to the job.

The previous two aces dealt with unspoken objections
and that advice applies here as well.

- **Legal difficulties:** In some states, you could be
  asked about criminal convictions. In other states,
  you can only be asked about convictions for a
  felony.

- **Personal Life:** An employer may not ask about
  your age, marital status or number of children.
  They may however ask about the date you
  graduated college, which is often a close proxy
  for age. Asking, "will you have any problem
  working long hours when necessary?" is permitted. **How** you will work long hours and take care
  of your children is not the employer's business.

You are permitted to raise these issues yourself, and

sometimes it may be to your advantage. For example, you may be relocating to live closer to a future spouse or significant other. Picture Beth interviewing for a position in Minnesota when she has lived her whole life in New England. "Why do you want to work in Minneapolis?", the interviewer asks. "I just love the Twin Cities" would be a weak response. Why not tell the truth? "I am involved in a serious relationship and we have decided to settle where he lives, namely Minnesota, rather than where I grew up." **Hint:** It's a bit more secure for both your life and the prospective employer's business if you can honestly say "I am getting married" rather than the more amorphous "serious relationship."

If you **are** asked an illegal question, what should you do? You have three options.

- **Answer the Question:** You could answer the question, particularly if your response addresses a concern about your ability to do the job. Some people would preface their response by saying "I am not sure why you are asking that, but..." or "I am not sure how that question relates to the job, but..."

- **Question the Question:** You could say "I am not sure why you are asking that question. Could you clarify for me in what way the subject is related to this job?" The interviewer may then gracefully back off, re-state the question appropriately or explain why the subject is essential to the job.

If you take this approach, understand that this is a delicate situation. Make sure you respond in a civil, non-confrontational tone.

- **Refuse to Answer:** You could say "I'm sorry but I believe that question is illegal, although you may not have intended it that way. As a matter of principle, I will not answer it."

I am not a lawyer and I encourage you to speak with a competent attorney **before** you start interviewing if these issues might affect you, especially disabilities or criminal record. But legal advice is not enough. You need to consider which of the approaches indicated above you wish to follow and then become comfortable with it. In that regard, you might want to speak with an employment counselor, a state employment representative or a human resource professional at a firm to which you will **not** be applying. In addition, if an employer asked an improper question, you should seriously consider the possibility that this would not be a good job to accept even if offered.

Where Are We Now?

In this chapter we looked at ways to deal with "objections" about your job candidacy, namely doubts about how well you fit the requirements of the job. We saw that objections could exist over a number of issues and that they are not always expressly stated.

In the next chapter, we will begin an extended examination of ways to ace questions you may be asked at your interview.

5

40 Sample Questions You Can Ace— Historical Questions

Different interviewers will ask different questions based on either their personal preference or company policy. However, all legitimate questions can be thought of as being either historical (past, present or future) or behavioral, although other terminology is sometimes used. Under historical, we could include questions about specific skills or technical abilities and how you acquired them. An interviewer will not say, "Here comes an historical question," or "This is a behavioral question." The point of identifying these two categories here is to help you prepare for both types of questions.

This chapter will deal with forty common historical questions. Behavioral questions are the subject of a separate chapter.

Validating

Sometimes you will be asked questions intended to clarify or validate items on your resume. A question like this can be utilized as a double win for you. First, since you are an expert on your resume you should have a solid base for a response. Second, you should welcome the opportunity to alleviate any doubts or concerns your interviewer may have. **Hint:** A good way to prepare for these kinds of questions is to have a friend ask you "how" and/or "why" about every line of your resume. This exercise in self reflection will prepare you to ace historical questions. It will also help you remember what is on your own resume, a common sense preparation that many people unfortunately ignore (See Exercise I at the end of this chapter).

Ace #41: Confirm Your Resume

You may be asked a question like this.

> Q.   "Sam, your resume indicates that you reduced the accounts receivable backlog at Formerco by 20%. How did you do that?"

Avoid getting entangled in explaining "what you really meant to say." Whether it was 19% or 21% is not really the issue. Also, the question didn't ask if the backlog reduction was by dollar volume or number of accounts, so no need to go into a lengthy expedition exploring the differences there. The question is probing to see if your resume is credible. Give an affirmative answer which goes straight to the point. Here's an example:

> A.   "I reduced the backlog by 20% by taking three steps. First I prioritized the receivables by age and amount. Second, I put accounts which had to be

handled with special diplomacy into a separate category because of the significant relationship involved. Third, I went after the small, but older accounts first since they were the ones most likely to become bad debts."

This answer confirms the credibility of your resume while also showing how your thought process works. **Hint:** Be prepared for a follow-up question like: "Why didn't you go after the big dollar accounts first?" Or "Do you think going after the smaller, older accounts rather than larger, newer accounts was a good idea?"

Doing It Badly

Sam could set back his chances by an ill-considered response.

"That 20% number was just an estimate. Anyhow, I was thinking about number of accounts, not dollar volume, so that 20% number is probably in the right ball park."

This is a weak start because Sam is spinning his wheels and conveying a feeling that he is uncomfortable with what he said on his own resume. Sam could proceed to dig his hole a little deeper by not telling much about **how** he reduced the backlog:

"It took a lot of hard work, that I remember."

Ace #42: Show the Significance of Context

Sometimes an historical or validating question needs to be put into context in order to have significance at your interview.

Q.   "George, I read on your resume that you resolved a dispute between labor and management at Humango Warehouse. What was the cause of that dispute?"

Let's say that the dispute was over cafeteria facilities. If you answer simply, "There was a dispute over cafeteria facilities," the interviewer is liable to miss the significance. Your job is to put the event into context so its significance will be clear. Here is a sample response:

A. "There was a dispute over the cafeteria. White collar employees were leaving for lunch 15 minutes early so they could grab the best tables. The blue collar workers had to wait for the noon whistle. This issue may seem minor, but the resentment of the blue collar workers was lowering morale and making labor-management relations that much tenser. I cleared the air by simply closing the cafeteria until 12:05. It was a simple solution which defused a growing problem."

Ace #43: Involuntary Termination

Q. "Jennifer, help me clarify something on your resume. When you left Cashin Corporation, did you start at Milcoworks right away?"

When bad news or awkward situations are involved, keep your answer short. It doesn't pay to hide the fact of an involuntary termination, but, don't dwell on the departure. Instead move quickly to the good news of landing the subsequent job.

A. "I got caught in a downsizing at Cashin. Fortunately, I have a good reputation in the field and was able to secure a new position in only a few weeks."

Or

A.   "No, there was an interval of about two months. My departure was unexpected, stemming from a change in the top management team. I had many friends in the industry helping me with the job search, so the search was relatively quick."

Doing It Badly

There are several ways to shoot yourself in the foot with this question. The most prominent are fudging and bad mouthing. Let's hope that Jennifer **doesn't** respond like this:

"Well, you know that times can be difficult. I was doing a great job, but with office politics and all, there wasn't much future at Formerco."

Or

"It's hard to believe about a successful company like Fomerco, but they have some insecure, paranoid managers. I got stuck working for one of them. Office politics counted for more than productivity so I got canned"

If Jennifer badmouths a previous company or supervisor she raises the fear she would be a badmouth at a new job as well.

It is also possible to give the interviewer the sense that it was poor performance rather than bad luck which led to your early exit:

"I couldn't believe that they let me go. I mean, I had more seniority than anybody else. I had my own way of doing things, so there was never any need for me to go to those time consuming training sessions. I always let people know what I was thinking. So why me?"

Jennifer should leave any anger or bitterness at home. A new employer will stay away from a malcontent and will not want to inherit any negativity you developed at a previous job.

Motivational Questions

A second category of historical questions probe your motivation for seeking a new job. Here are three typical motivation questions. Be prepared for each. **Your motivation may be as important as your skills in determining whether you get the job offer.**

Ace #44: Why Do You Want to Leave Your Current Employer?

If you are currently employed, a reasonable question is "Why do you want to leave your current employer?" The key here is to say something nice about your current job and then move straight to a discussion of what attracts you to the situation for which you are interviewing. Don't dwell on the literal wording of the question (i.e. "Why do you want to **leave?**") since negative comments about your current situation can't help you win the next job offer. Your response could be something like this:

"I have had a good experience with my current employer. While there, I have managed situations from the mundane to the critical and have grown in each case. My interest in your firm is based on the challenge of the job we're discussing today and your firm's commitment to growth through excellence."

Even if your job search is involuntary, stay focused on the next step. For example "I had a good experience at Formerco. Unfortunately, there was a downsizing and I got caught in it. The reason I am interested in Yourco is..."

Doing It Badly

This book suggests in several places keeping your answers short and not dwelling on the literal wording of a question, especially in awkward situations. The purpose is to avoid sinking into a morass of muddy subjects that don't help your candidacy.

Here is the type of response to avoid:

"I want to leave my current employer because there's no challenge left. Each tomorrow ends up being a lot like yesterday. Besides, business is terrible and everybody is in an awful mood. I need a change."

Ace #45: Why Should We Hire You?

Most of the questions you will be asked at a job interview are intended to probe a single mega-question: "Should this company offer this applicant the job?" It would be reasonable to ask you that question directly and explicitly, perhaps like this:

> Q. "George, why should we hire you?"

Although this question may seem intimidating, you actually laid the groundwork for an answer with Aces 3 and 4. There, you anticipated the needs of the company and prepared examples to show that you offer what the company needs. Based on the chart you prepared then, you can now give the employer several good reasons to hire you.

> A. "There are several skills you need in a market researcher and I have demonstrated them through my past experience. Let me give you several examples. In terms of research, while at Sourceco I researched potential suppliers in terms of location, quality and price. At Consumerco I analyzed consumer purchasing patterns. I developed my writing skills working for my college newspaper and used them effectively at Consumerco. In a similar way, I developed presentation skills in college class projects and used them making presentations about spring vacation packages in fraternities and sororities."

The interviewer is likely to follow-up with a question about George's experience at Consumerco or Sourceco.

Ace #46: Why Do You Want to Work For Us?

As important as your skills for doing the job is your reason for wanting it. The winning response will give specific reasons why you want **that job** for **that firm**.

Q. "John, why do you want to work for us?"

A. "The first reason has to do with the job. It seems to involve a good deal of what I am looking for, namely an analytical position in a team work environment. Frankly, I like the people I have met who work here and that's important to me. Also, I am impressed that this firm has an open door management style and has achieved five straight years of growth."

If it's true, John could add an attraction related to the firm's industry. "My last reason is an interest to the widget industry. I've been following it for several years from an avocational perspective. I continue to find the subject of widgets and their role in American life interesting."

Did You Come Prepared?

Remember two of our basic interview principles: An interview is a *business meeting between equals* and *be yourself at your best*. A fundamental question in any employer's mind is "Do you come to a meeting (or other work situation) prepared?" Being prepared is part of being at your best. Here are two common "are you prepared?" questions (see page 65):

Doing It Badly

There are several truly awful ways John could have responded about his reasons for wanting the job. Unfortunately each of these is heard in interviews of real people who are probably putting a torpedo into their chance of getting the job offer.

A. "Look, I need a job, right?"

Hint: Desperation has no friends.

A. "You have a big company with lots of opportunity."

Hint: Your answers should reflect research and serious thought. Bigness may be a fact, but why is it a factor for you?

A. "You offer free employee parking and great benefits."

Hint: Fringe benefits are a fringe issue until the job is offered.

Here are other self destructive answers people sometimes give. Would you hire someone who gave you an answer like this?

- I hear you guys have summer hours and I want my Friday afternoons off.

- Because of your retirement plan.

- This job is close to where I live.

- I just want to see what's out there.

- I need a few years of experience to get into a good MBA program.

- This job is my foot in the door. I hope to move to another function in a year or so.

A short parable may be in order.

John wanted a date for a dance on Saturday night. He saw Mary walking down the street. "Will you go to the dance with me?" John asked. "Why are you inviting me, John?" responded Mary. "I need to go with somebody and luckily you came by!" John exclaimed.

Ace #47: Know About the Company

Q: "Tell me what you know about our company."

A six to eight sentence response touching upon major facts such as products, size, recent performance and related news events would be the heart of a terrific answer. Since you should already have researched the company (see Ace 2), you already have the raw material for a response.

A. "I studied Yourco's annual report and some of the promotional literature designed for potential customers. Yourco's recent growth rate of 16% annually over the last five years is really impressive. Of the firm's three divisions, widgets and gadgets have been particularly successful. The gizmo division has been just breaking even though. The chairman, Ted Young, has announced that he plans to grow the company to a $250,000 million firm by the year 2,000, mostly by deeper penetration of existing markets."

Ace #48: Challenges

Part of being prepared is knowing how the firm sees present and future business challenges. Anticipate a question like this: "What challenges do you think this firm is going to face over the next five years?" A good response will show that you have done your research (again, see Ace 2) **and** that you can be an asset in meeting those challenges. Your answer could start something like this:

A. "The biggest challenge for any firm in this industry is being positioned properly to deliver high quality products at competitive prices. This will be increasingly difficult because technology is changing both what is in demand and the cost-effective methods of manufacturing the product rapidly. The last five years have shown that trying to predict even the nature of future changes can be dicey, to say the least."

If you are experienced in the field you could add, "During my three years at Similarco, I helped the firm navigate some choppy waters by instituting a careful review of capital expenditures which might lock us in to an uncompetitive posture."

On the other hand, if you are trying to transfer your talents to a new industry, you might continue, "At companies like Nowco, we face a similar dilemma, although it's not as pronounced. The lead time needed to design and manufacture a product can be 18 months. The consumer market can turn 180 degrees in that time. I have been instrumental in negotiating strategic partnerships which have eased our capital constraints and connected us to larger markets."

Ace #49: Most/Least Questions

You may be asked a question phrased in the superlative:

Q. "Herman, describe the best (worst) manager you ever had."

As a first step, Herman may want to reframe the question for himself to "describe a good (or bad) manager you had." Thought of this way, there is no need to literally rank every manager Herman ever had. Then he can address the general intent of the question without trying to remember if Gene Green was the best, or merely good.

A. "One of the managers that I learned a lot from

was Gene Green at Formerco. Gene knew how to get the most out of his staff by being demanding but reasonable at the same time. Applying the lessons I learned from Gene has helped me become a good manager at Nowco."

What Herman has done here is describe **a** good manager in terms of some of the things Herman gained from him. That's a positive step. Herman also kept his answer short. If he waxed exuberant on the subject, he might describe someone very **unlike** his prospective next boss. That wouldn't be helpful to Herman's cause.

What if the question had been framed in the **negative?** Side stepping the superlative "worst" is still in order, but there is the additional taboo against badmouthing a past manager or employer. You could give a response like this:

A. "Actually, I have been very fortunate. Each of the three bosses I have had were good managers. Unfortunately one did get distracted because of a painful personal situation, and I think that limited his effectiveness."

The Hypothetical

You may be asked a hypothetical question introduced by a phrase like "What would you do if...?" There are three ways to ace a hypothetical question.

Ace #50: Actualize the Hypothetical

One way to deal with a hypothetical question is to discuss an actual situation. This approach is easier for some people because it is less abstract. An actual example may also be more meaningful to the interviewer.

Your answer may begin like this: "I was in a situation like

that once. Let me tell you how I handled it."

Ace #51: It Wouldn't Happen Because; Thought Process

It is possible that you will be asked about a hypothetical situation you would work hard to prevent. For example:

Q. "Samantha, tell me what you would do if you had two deadlines to meet simultaneously and had time to complete only one."

A. "That situation doesn't happen to me because I always put my ducks in a row long before a deadline looms. Let me give you an example."

Another possible response to a hypothetical question is to show your **thought process.** For example: "In order to deal with that situation, the first thing I would need to know would be..."

Ace #52: Handling Comparisons

Comparison questions can be difficult because you are liable to get enmeshed in negatives, and that won't help your cause. Let's look at some potential comparison questions and how to respond.

Q. "Becky, as you know communication skills are very important in this business. Do you see yourself as being stronger in written or oral communication?"

A question probing your oral and written skills is perfectly legitimate. However, you need to make sure that your response doesn't put down one skill at the expense of the other. At the same time, you don't have to be equally talented in both skills. I suggest an answer like this:

A. "I realize that both oral and written communication are important. My presentations at team meetings are good and I give direct, concise answers when probed by more senior managers. Still, I think my written skills are better, judged by the fact that I am the informal resource utilized for writing correspondence and proposals."

The comparison could be between you and other applicants for the job.

Q. "David, why should I hire you rather than someone who has more experience in our industry?"

Focus on your strengths. Any reference to others should be brief and respectful. You could start out like this:

A. "This is an exciting job opportunity and I'm sure that you will have many high quality applicants. The reason you should hire me is..."

Hint: You might even want to turn the implied objection into an asset: "The fact that my experience is in a different industry could be a plus for Yourco because I bring with me a fresh perspective."

Another type of comparison could be between two employers.

Q. "Linda, how would you compare Thisco to Thatotherco. with which you are interviewing?"

A. "I mentioned earlier that I am interviewing with Thatotherco. As far as I can tell, it is well managed and generates most of its revenue from consumer products. Thisco is a little smaller, but enjoys better margins on its products because they are high-end impulse items. One of the things that originally got me interested in Thisco is your ability to identify products which attract consumer demand, but not competition, at least for the short run."

If you are asked to compare your current employer to Thisco, be especially careful to speak no evil. I suggest sticking to publicly available facts like size, structure and product line.

The Sucker Punches

Some interviewers will ask you to provide negative information about yourself. This is not the time for some cleansing catharsis. Negative information will be held against you. The key is to parry the potential blow without explicitly ducking the question.

First let's look at three aces to deal with the dreaded weaknesses question.

Weaknesses

Q. "Ralph, you've told me about some of your strengths. Now tell me about your weaknesses. Everybody has some."

You can't win anything on this question. The best you can do is neutralize it. Here are three aces for dealing with a question about your weaknesses.

Ace #53: The Classic

The Classic approach is to discuss a strength, but label it a weakness. For example:

> "I tend to be very concerned about deadlines, so I make sure that I have all my assignments done early. I know that I can't expect that from everyone."

Or

> "I have higher expectations of myself than my manager has of me. I know not to demand higher than established standards from others."

A word of caution. Be careful not to reveal an actual weakness accidentally. It's fine to say, "I work hard and effectively to finish all my projects on time." However, it would be destructive to say "I tend to be a workaholic" since that term connotes a characteristic which can be a real weakness in many situations. Similarly, note that the examples given here indicate that you don't expect everyone to live up to your higher than needed standards. An overly demanding employee can cause problems with other employees in the organization.

There is an alternate form of the classic response which is applicable for some people. Let's say that you are weak in a skill area that is important to the job. A response showing how you are **overcoming or compensating** for that weakness makes sense because it needs to be addressed during the interview. For example: "My computer skills are not up to speed yet. I am taking an evening course in computers and have been asking for more assignments involving computer use at my current job."

Ace #54: The Trivalizer

Another approach is to respond with something which is plausibly a weakness but is so unconnected to the immediate context it probably won't hurt you. For example: "I have never been very good at the natural sciences."

That would certainly be true of me, as my college transcript will attest. However, you may be able to minimize even a trivial weakness. "I keep up with the sciences through articles in the general press, but when it gets to the highly technical aspects, it's beyond me." The general press is available to us all!

Of course you want to make sure that the weakness really is trivial. Natural sciences may not be critical to an accountant, but this weakness would not be trivial for a chemist.

When you respond with the Classic or the Trivializer, might the interviewer feel that you are playing games? Of course! But this is a games playing question. The name of this game is "Will the Job Candidate Self-Destruct?" It is within the rules to say "no."

Let's say that the interviewer is relentless in the pursuit of your weaknesses: "Robert, you have given me a 'weakness' which is really a strength and a weakness which would be trivial in our context. Come on now, tell me a real weakness."

The rules of the game have not changed, namely don't testify against yourself. Instead, it is time to respond with the ultimate ace for a weakness question: The Comeback.

Ace #55: The Comeback

Remember, you want to parry the blow without explicitly ducking the question. Now is the time to respond calmly with The Comeback. "I certainly want to address your question. What potential weaknesses are you concerned about?"

Stated this way, you are telling the interviewer to define his or her concerns. This is a lot safer for you than trying to address weaknesses in an open ended response. In fact, if you become comfortable with The Comeback, it could be your first response to a weaknesses question.

The Comeback may have an additional advantage for you: The interviewer may identify potential objections that might otherwise have gone unexpressed (See Chapter 4).

Some interviewers may feel put on the defensive by a Comeback response. Several corporate human resource professionals expressed precisely this concern to me when they read this chapter. In my view, asking someone to clarify their point is in keeping with the business meeting between equals nature of the interview. This is especially true when that person has felt **free to ask** you any legal question s/he felt appropriate. However, if the Comeback makes you feel uncomfortable, stick with the Classic or the Trivalizer.

Ace #56: Choose Life (Not Poison or Hanging)

These are other potential sucker punches. For example "Would you rather work for a man or a woman?"

Avoid choosing between unacceptable options in a multiple choice situation. For example, would you prefer to die by poison or hanging? Your answer would be, "Actually I prefer to live." Similarly, the gender of your manager is irrelevant, so step outside the choices given: "To me the gender of the person I work for is irrelevant." You could add if true "I have worked well for both men and women in the past." In the early 1960's, during the Cold War, the late President John Kennedy was asked if he would rather "Be Dead or Red." President Kennedy responded that we shall be both alive and free.

Ace #57: Guard Proprietary Information

You may be asked for information relating to a current or past employer that is proprietary, that is, property of the firm which it chooses to safeguard from competitors or the public. If you are asked a question of that nature respond with a general answer which clearly indicates you will not reveal proprietary information.

> Q. "John what type of research projects were you involved in at Onceco?"

> A. "Because of the proprietary nature of that research, I can only tell you that I was engaged in finding new uses for polymers." If John revealed specifics of his research, he would be betraying a trust. He would also undermine his own chances for the new job. Nobody loves people with loose lips or suspect loyalty.

Stress Questions

Horror stories are still told about stress interview situations. A job candidate might be asked to open a window which was nailed shut or be addressed in a clearly confrontational tone. Fortunately, these situations are not common today because they don't yield worthwhile results and are generally considered unprofessional. However if you find yourself in a stress situation, there are three avenues open to you. In all three cases remember that a stress question is really a reflection on the interviewer, so don't take it personally.

In the case of Ace 59 or Ace 60, the response suggested is appropriate only if you are so offended that preserving your dignity is worth the risk of not getting the job offer. That is a personal decision only you can make.

Ace #58: Play the Game

Once you realize that a stress question is a game (albeit an ill considered one), you could decide to play the game while holding your ground. For example:

Interviewer: "Louis, I think your tie is ugly."

Louis: "I happen to like this tie and I am sorry that you don't. If you hire me, I will buy a new one!"

Ace #59: Where is This Question Coming From?

A more assertive response would be to ask why the question is being asked in such a harsh tone, or indeed why is it being asked at all.

Interviewer (stated in a demeaning tone): "This is an important job in an important company. Why would a person with your limited experience even bother to apply for it?"

George: "I can understand why you would ask about my experience in relation to this job, and I would be glad to tell you. But first I must tell you that I felt that the tone of your question made me feel uncomfortable."

Stated this way, you have made clear that you will not be bullied. At the same time you have given the interviewer a chance to back-off. It is to your advantage to give the interviewer the benefit of the doubt and you have nothing to gain by backing him/her into a corner.

Ace #60: Walk Out

If you feel that you can't give a controlled response like the two already indicated, you could decide to walk out. Perhaps you could simply say, "I feel that the offensive nature of your question makes it impossible to continue this interview." That approach may preserve your dignity. It may even preserve a chance at getting the job.

The latter point may seem surprising, but let's consider it. The job for which you interviewed might still be a good one even if the interviewer behaved like an oaf with an attitude. When you are sure you are composed, I suggest asking the hiring manager or other senior official to schedule an interview for another day. Be prepared to discuss the rudeness you experienced, if asked. That should start an interesting examination of what happened. Since you left without saying a single harsh word, no one will be able to muddy the waters and implicate you in the interview's demise. Will you get another interview? Not necessarily. But if the job is potentially worth having, the extra effort to get it is worth doing.

The Present: Your Current Job

Since your past and present serve as predictors for your future, it makes sense to ask about your current job. This is a topic you should know well and one that puts some of your other answers in context. Let's look at some questions about your current job you should be prepared to ace.

Ace #61: What You Enjoy

A question like "What do you enjoy most (or least) about your current job?" would be one way the interviewer could initiate this topic. Here are a few guidelines to keep in mind before answering:

- Don't take words like "most" or "least" literally. In this example, mention something that you enjoy without worrying if it is really on the top of your list.

- If it's a "least" question, make sure you don't badmouth your current firm or previous supervisors. You also don't want to identify aspects which are important in your prospective job.

- If it's a combination "most and least," focus on the positive.

    Q. "Max, what aspects of your current job do you like most and which do you like least?"

    A. "I am generally happy with my current job. I enjoy the team work, the variety and the firm's commitment to excellence. The firm's relative smallness means that upward movement is limited so I wish Nowco were about 50% larger."

Hint: If this question was the opener, Max should make sure to include at least one of his positive attitudes. For example:

    A. "I like Nowco. It offers a team work environment, variety and a commitment to excellence. I also like combining my analytical and interpersonal skills."

Ace #62: Ace Your Current Situation

The interviewer may want to gain an understanding of the structure of your current job. This would give her/him a better context for asking questions and for evaluating the answers you give.

The key here is to be honest and upbeat. Tell the facts as they are, briefly. Of course you could add a note about why you were promoted into your current position or some of the talent you have developed while there.

    Q. "Aaron, tell me about your current job. I am particularly interested in knowing what your reporting relationships are."

Let's assume that Aaron is interviewing for a position which would be a step up.

A. "I report to the Director of Operations. In fact, I replaced her in my current position. Day to day, I work with the sales force and the production people to make sure that our delivery commitments and manufacturing process are 'in sync.' From being in a hands on position, I have gained a thorough grasp of operations, including the politics and cost aspects. I learned a good deal about effective management from my boss."

Aaron's response is to the point and gives the interviewer some good topics to follow-up. They are topics which show Aaron growing towards the level of the job for which he is applying.

Aaron has not embellished on his responsibilities or given any misleading impressions. A dishonest answer is unethical. In addition, if you are caught in a lie, including exaggeration or shading the truth, it is likely to cost you the job.

Ace #63: Current Job and Our Job

You should expect to hear a question like this:

Q. "David, do you think the work you have done at Nowco has prepared you for this job at Ourco?"

The general theme of David's answer will be "yes, let me give you some particulars." David might also mention some of his attributes that are of value to Ourco which aren't connected to his current job. Examples might be facility with foreign languages or public speaking.

A. "Yes, I do. At Nowco I have established a track record of reducing costs, increasing clients and staying ahead of the competition. I have done this by developing a productive staff and keeping lines of communication open. All of this is important to Ourco, even though Nowco and Ourco are in different industries. In addition, I remain conversant in Spanish, a language I have kept up with since graduating from college. I have developed my public speaking skills as a member of the Chamber of Commerce's speakers bureau."

Ace #64: Recent Performance Review

An interviewer might ask you some pointed questions about a recent performance review. Presented this way, you would seem to have less latitude than a generic strengths/weaknesses question. Let's think about this for a moment. You have every right to consider your performance evaluation to be a matter between you and your boss. On the other hand, this is probably not the time to make a broad case for privacy rights. Instead I suggest these steps: Start by discussing things for which you were commended. Next mention something your boss wants you to improve and indicate what you are doing in that regard. If the needs-to-be-improved is connected to a potential promotion, it would be helpful to say so.

Q. "Myrna, let's get specific about strengths and weaknesses. What did your manager say about you in your last performance review?"

A. "My manager, Barry Mellini, identified a number

of accomplishments, especially the increases in productivity that I mentioned earlier. Barry noted my work ethic, communication skills and decision making even under stress. He did suggest that I gain greater facility with our new computer network and I am utilizing it more in my projects now."

Myrna stressed the positive, mentioning an area she is improving. What if the question pointedly refers to negatives? There is no point in volunteering ammunition which could be used against you, but suggesting that there were no negatives at all would be hard to believe.

Q.   "Myrna, did Barry Young mention any negatives about your performance in the review?"

A.   "As I mentioned, there were things to work on, like our computer system. A second was to make more extensive use of audio-visual props in making presentations."

If Myrna senses that some particular weakness may be of concern, she could add: "I want to make sure that I am answering your question. Are there specific concerns that you have?"

Responding this way, Myrna invites the interviewer to probe any negatives, and being open is a positive characteristic. Unfortunately, some interviewers may feel defensive about Myrna's question, so she should ask it only if she senses a remaining need to dispel doubts about a potential weakness.

Ace #65: Balanced Retrospective

Shakespeare said "never did the course of true love run smooth." That sentiment probably applies to most careers as well. An interviewer may ask you to look over your past as a means of understanding your present and gaining a sense of what your values for the future are.

> Q. "Ann, you've been in the work force for about ten years since graduating college. As you look back on that period, how would you assess your career so far?"

Because Ann has anticipated a question like this, she knows that there are some guidelines to follow. First, if she is unhappy with her current situation, she shouldn't show too much of that. Nobody loves a whiner. Second, there is no need to act as though she had experienced no bumps on the career road. Ann could give an answer like this one:

> A. "I feel fortunate to have a good work situation now. Still, sometimes I think it might have been even better if I had taken a different approach early-on and asked for more risky assignments. It took me a while to build my self confidence to the point where I can ask for the type of assignments which will move me along faster in Nowco."

Ann's response is that things are fine now, but perhaps they could have been even better. She accepts full responsibility for the way her career has developed and doesn't badmouth others.

What if Ann's career had been hurt by circumstances beyond her control like a corporate bankruptcy or reorganization? Ann should consider such events as unfortunate and go on from there. "Unfortunately, my career progress was interrupted when Formerco filed for Chapter 11 and downsized about half the staff. It took me a while to land a position at Nowco and of course it takes some time to prove yourself again in a new company. On the other hand landing on my feet actually strengthened my self-confidence while making me more sensitive to other people's sense of job insecurity."

Or

"When Formerco went into Chapter 11, it downsized half its staff and my job was eliminated. At first I was devastated, losing my job and daily contact with people I really liked. But, I started a job search and found a wonderful position at Nowco. In a sense, being laid-off actually helped my career because my new job introduced me to new responsibilities in an industry which is still growing."

Managerial Style

Ace #66: When You Hired Someone

If you are (or were) in a position to hire others, a question about your criteria and process would make a lot of sense. Your response will reveal something about how you relate to staff and to the larger goals of your organization. The keys here are: Show a clear, reasonable basis for the decision you made; indicate that you looked for both talent and the fit with the overall goals of the organization. Avoid showing a managerial style which is inconsistent with that of your prospective new employer.

Q. "Jeff, you mentioned that you have a staff of ten reporting to you. What did you look for in the last person you hired (or, what would you look for if you were hiring someone next week)?"

A.   "I have hired two people recently, and interviewed several others as part of a panel. Talent is a base line consideration for me. Considering their past performance, could they do the job for us? I am also concerned about fit with the rest of my staff and other people they work with. Not that I want clones. I just want to avoid Lone Rangers and abrasive characters. Promotability is also an issue, because I don't want to hire people who will stagnate."

Ace #67: In Your Boss's Shoes

Two of the reasons people seek new jobs are salvation (they need to leave their current one) and advancement (they see an opportunity to advance their career). Either way, it makes sense to ask what you would do in your boss's shoes. In the first instance, the question would probe your true situation at your current job. In the second case, the question would elicit a picture of how your mind might work in a higher position.

Your response operates within two parameters. The first is familiar, namely **never** badmouth anybody. The second is that you don't want to seem to be your boss's clone.

Q.   "Judy, if you were in your boss's shoes, what would you do differently than s/he does?"

Judy pauses before responding. She remembers not to take the question so literally as to focus on the word "differently." At the same time, she takes account of the parameters we have noted and gives an answer like this:

A.   "I have learned a lot from my boss, Alvin Conifer. He is dedicated to his job, has contributed to the firm's success and understands the people he works with. His managerial style tends to be a bit more controlling than mine might be, but that may reflect the general style of Nowco."

The interviewer might follow-up by asking:

Q. "Can you be a bit more specific about what you would do differently?"

Judy realizes that the general parameters for her response remain the same. If she is aware of the managerial imperatives or taboos of Yourco (but most people probably aren't) she will take that into account. Her response must now elaborate a bit more on what Judy would do differently. For example:

A. "I mentioned that Alvin tends to be more directly controlling than I think I would be in his position. My tendency would be to give staff members more independent decision making. I think the gains in creativity would outweigh possible losses from a looser guiding hand."

Ace #68: Your Subordinates

Another way of probing your managerial skill is asking how those you manage would describe you. Let's assume first that you do manage others. There's no reason to believe that everyone is ready to fall on their sword for you. On the other hand, most people should at least respect you and have an appropriate degree of professional loyalty. With those boundaries in mind, here's how the question might be played out.

Q. "Dorothy, how do you think your subordinates would describe you if I guaranteed them ironclad anonymity?"

A. "Well, I hope they wouldn't really feel any need to protect their identity, but I know what you mean. I think most of my staff, that's about 20 people, would describe me as demanding but fair. They would recognize that I try to help each one advance his/her own career through challenging assignments and appropriate training sessions. Communication is a two way street and I am also open to new ideas. At the same time, major decisions are ultimately my responsibility and not determined by majority vote."

Not by coincidence, Dorothy has her subordinates describing her much as she would describe herself. Notice that Dorothy did not say that her **entire** staff felt this way or that people love her more than their own mother.

Every answer could give birth to another question, so Dorothy should be ready for a follow-up question to probe possible negatives.

Q. "You spoke about what **most** of your subordinates would say. Are there some who would mention some negatives?"

It's hard to imagine a work place where never is heard a discouraging word. On the other hand, it won't help to amplify on the points of discontent.

A. "Yes, there are a few employees who would have negatives to mention. One is upset that I didn't recommend him for a choice assignment. Another would like her ideas adopted more often. I am proud to be respected by the vast majority of my staff, but I don't expect adulation or unanimous support."

Ace #69: Putting Out Fires

In almost every profession, there are at least occasional situations which arise suddenly and require immediate attention. A question about these "fires" and how you put them out can be expected. It probes both the kind of situations you have faced and the kind of steps you took to address them.

Q. "Janice, most jobs present us with some fires to be put out. Tell about a fire you recently dealt with."

A. "To use the fire-fighting metaphor, the first thing I do is take fire prevention seriously and have a system operating that will put a fire out if it gets started. Let me be specific. A potential fire would be the late delivery of a critical part by a subcontractor. I insist on progress reports so that our needs don't go on their back burner. In addition, I also have at least two subcontractors for each component so we're not completely dependent on any one of them.

"To contain a fire, I develop contingency plans including possible changes in production schedules and prioritizing our customer deliveries. Would you like me to tell you more about that?"

Ace #70: Handling Disappointment/Rejection

In every job, there are some times of disappointment. Perhaps it was a recommendation not accepted, a project which failed to meet objectives, a potential deal which didn't go through. A productive employee should learn something from the situation without becoming demoralized.

Q. "Michael, what was your biggest professional disappointment and how did you handle it?"

Before responding, Michael remembers to take several things into account. First, he doesn't have to rank order his disappointments to identify the one which was literally the biggest. Second, he must be careful not to badmouth anyone in connection with the disappointment. Third, he wants to show what he learned from the situation.

A. "When I first came to Nowco, I put a tremendous amount of energy into a proposal for cutting operating costs. When senior management rejected it, I felt terribly disappointed.

"Where had I gone wrong? I thought about it and also discussed the proposal's fate with my boss. It turned out to be a good learning experience because I came to understand that even a sound proposal may be outweighed by other or greater factors. The good news is that the senior managers appreciated my initiative and thoroughness in making the proposal and have been open to recommendations that I have made since then."

In some situations like sales, rejection is intrinsic to the job. You are more likely to hear "no" than "yes" in any given situation. If Michael were interviewing for a situation of that type, his answer would change.

A. "Rejection is part of the job. The important thing is to learn from the situation if you can and go on to the next call in any case. I make a lot of cold calls, and I close on maybe one out of fifty! Two percent closed deals is considered good in my business and I don't let the 98% which are rejections get in my way."

Ace #71: Where Else Are You Looking?

Let's assume that Jack and Jan are engaged. If Jack asks: "Who else are you seeing, Jan?" we hope that the answer is "There is no one else, honey. We're engaged."

The interview process is **not** like that. You have every right to interview with many potential employers, just as the company will probably interview many different job applicants. So what do you do with a question like:

Q. "Allan, what other companies are you hoping to interview with?"

The point of the question is to determine how serious and well directed your job search is. This is a legitimate question. Give a straight forward, non-defensive answer. For example, if Thisco is the **only** firm you are interviewing with, you could say:

A. "I am being very selective about where I send my resume. Right now, Thisco is the only firm with which I am interviewing. I pursued this opportunity because I am impressed by your company's success in anticipating market demand. Also, I believe this job is a good fit with my skills and goals."

This response answers the question and lays the groundwork for a follow-up question about Allan's motivation for seeking a job at Thisco.

On the other hand, maybe you are seeking interviews with a number of firms. There is no reason to hide that, as long as there is some consistency to the nature of the jobs and/or industry.

A.   "I am very glad to be here today, because I am
     very interested in the position we are discussing.
     However, I am also applying for similar positions
     in a number of other firms (**or** I am also applying to
     other firms in the industry)."

No matter how you respond, be prepared for a follow-up
question like this:

Q.   "What can you tell me about the kind of opportuni-
     ties you decided not to pursue?"

This question would test whether you were really being
"very selective," as opposed to being not terribly energetic
in your job search.

Or

Q.   "You mentioned that you are pursuing a number
     of opportunities and that's fine. Who else have you
     interviewed with so far?"

This question would test how consistent your search
targets are. It might also probe your success rate at being
invited to interview. You could respond something like this:

A.   "I have applied to five similar situations. So far,
     this is my first interview."

Your Future With the Firm

Historical questions could also relate to your potential
future with the firm. (Warning: These questions don't mean
you are about to be offered the job!) These questions are

a way of testing your values, your sense of reality and your career goals.

Doing Things Differently

We said earlier that one reason for asking about your past is to use it as a predictor for your future. Asking you to see yourself in a future situation is also very informative. Here are five future oriented questions.

Ace #72: Describe How You Learn From Experience

Be prepared for a question about how you might do things differently in the future than you did in the past. When asked about doing things differently, reframe the question in your mind to "What did I learn from that experience and how have I acted differently since (or how would I act differently in the future)."

There are several circumstances where this could arise. Let's start with one of the most awkward.

> Q. "Robin, it seems that you had some problems dealing with people on your last job. If you could do it over again, what would you do differently?"

Let's assume that there were some interpersonal problems at Robin's last job. Robin should focus on what she gained from that experience which might make her a good employee on her next job. Robin should understand that this question could rebound to her benefit if she answers it well.

> A. "I did a lot of soul searching on that very question. In fact, I asked some of my friends from work for help with it. What I learned is to separate my

personal self from my professional self. If there was a harsh question, for example, it was not aimed at me personally, but related to something I needed to accomplish in the professional realm.

"I have been working through a temporary agency in the three months since I left Formerco. According to my exit interviews, my interpersonal relationships have been excellent on both work sites to which I was assigned."

A less pointed form of the question could be this:

Q. "Aaron, as you look over the last ten years, are there some career decisions you wish you had made differently?"

A. "I think that I have been successful in building a rewarding career in this field. At the same time, I have thought about choices I made and paths not taken. Since I feel happy with my career, I don't have major regrets. However, I think I might be further along if I hadn't been able to focus on the technical career path a lot earlier."

Ace #73: What Part of This Job Wouldn't You like?

Avoid the extremes of fishing for something not to like or stating that this job would put you in career heaven. Pick something which is not central to the job and then add that everybody finds something in their job which doesn't excite them.

Doing It Badly

Imagine where Robin or Aaron would be if they had given answers like this to a question about doing things differently.

A. "Next time I will be more careful about choosing the people I work with. You only lose when you work with losers."

Or

A. "I am looking for a job where people do what I say because its me who said it. None of this 'touchy-feely' stuff for me!"

Or

A. "I am sorry I ever left my job at Onceco to accept that position at Formerco. I gave up a cushy job and ended up in a company that didn't

Q. "Ann, there must be some part of this job you wouldn't like. Tell me about it."

A. "Based on some informational meetings I had with people at Yourco, I think that the decision making process at Yourco may be a little slower than I am used to now. That's something I need to get used to. Also, I like the engineers and factory workers at Nowco. I'm going to miss that element of diversity here."

Doing It Badly

Disliking **too much** of the job would be a real barrier to getting hired.

A. "I love the thought of being a stock broker, but I hate cold calling and time pressures."

What this answer says is: "I want the perceived glamour and money, but I don't like what I would need to do to get there."

Ace #74: What Will You Do If You Don't Come to Work Here?

Q. "Ann, let's suppose for a moment that we don't offer you a job. What do you see as your next career step?"

A. "Of course I would be disappointed because this job appeals to me very much. On the other hand I would still have my current job."

Let's freeze frame Ann's answer for a moment. How Ann continues depends on what she has already said (or would plan to say) about her current job. Ann might say, "As I mentioned earlier, that is a satisfactory situation at least for the short run."

Or

"Since I know that I am speaking in confidence, let me add that I would keep my eyes open for another excellent opportunity like this one."

If Ann is currently out of work she could say:

A. "I am looking for an excellent opportunity like the one we are discussing today. This type of job and this industry still seem to be an attractive fit for me, so that's where I would concentrate my efforts."

Ace #75: First Day on the Job

Everybody proclaims their eagerness to hit the ground running, make an immediate contribution, etc. One way to probe behind the buzz words is to ask a question like this.

Doing It Badly

Ann wouldn't give answers like these and neither should you:

A. "I guess I would just stay where I am until something better comes along."

A. "I am pinning my hopes on this job. If it falls through, I don't know exactly what I will do."

A. "Why aren't you going to offer me the job?"

Q.   "Shirley, let's assume for a moment that we do offer you a job and that you accept it. Describe for me what your first day on the job would be."

A.   "I hope that I would have a chance to speak with my manager before then to see what her priorities would be. But let me assume for a moment that it's purely a matter for my own discretion.

   "The first thing I would want to do is to meet with my staff and get a better sense of who they are and how they see things. It's important to show that I am not intent on imposing my style and structure just because they have been successful somewhere else. Then I would like to get re-acquainted with the other managers who were part of my interview process."

Make sure your "first day on the job" answer matches the way you plan to describe your managerial or work style. The answer Shirley gave here makes sense for a person who has highlighted (or will highlight) relationships with staff and peers. Had Shirley answered that she would start by clearing up left over paper work she would have shown priorities inconsistent with the needs of this job and the professed significance she attaches to interpersonal relations.

Ace #76: How Will You Evaluate Your Job Offers?

One way to probe your values is to ask how you would evaluate job offers you might receive. (Remember, this is not a hint that you are actually about to receive a job offer.) I suggest the following process both to prepare for this question and to use for the time when you do have an offer to evaluate.

1. Identify 5-7 attributes that a job should have to make you happy.

2. Divide 100 points among those attributes, allocating the most points to the most important attribute, the next most points to the next most important, etc. This will result in a rank ordered list against which you would evaluate a job. Here is a hypothetical example:

Lauren's Next Job	
Attributes	Importance Points
Challenging Work	30
Compensation	25
Advancement Opportunity	30
Compatible Co-workers	10
Balance of Work/Personal Life	5
	100
Gabrielle's Next Job	
Challenging Work	20
Compensation	10
Advancement Opportunity	10
Compatible Co-workers	25
Balance of Work/Personal Life	35
	100

In this example, Lauren clearly has an intense career focus in what she wants. Lauren has allocated 85 points to the nature of the professional challenge, compensation and advancement opportunity. Her friend Gabrielle wants the same attributes, but has a significantly different set of priorities. Gabrielle shows this by allocating 60 points to compatible co-workers and balanced life. A third friend, Marilyn, might have a completely different set of priorities.

3. Prepare an honest answer which doesn't tell more than is helpful.

Q. "Lauren, how are you going to evaluate your job offers?"

A. "The most important considerations for me are professional challenge, opportunity for advance-ment and competitive compensation. One of my attractions to Yourco is the challenge of dealing with shifting market demands and your commit-ment to keeping your employees on the cutting edge of the industry's advances."

Gabrielle might answer, "For me, a professional challenge being met by a group of professionals who like working together is important. In fact, part of my interest in Thisco is based upon your reputation as a good place to work and a firm that wants employees to be tops in the field while still having a life of their own."

It is possible that an employer might be equally inter-ested in both Lauren and Gabrielle. After all, the bottom line question is the applicant's ability to add value to the organization. However two things might change.

First, the probable follow-up questions for Lauren would be along the lines of "What do you find challenging now?" or "What part of this job do you think would challenge you?" or "How would this job fit into your longer term career plans?" For Gabrielle, follow-up questions are more likely to be "What type of balance between work life and personal life would you find ideal? Realistic?" or "Tell me about your current relationship with co-workers." Of course the follow-up questions might also be about what Lauren and Gabrielle found less important. For example, "Lauren why do you rate compatible co-workers as less important than compensation?" or "Gabrielle, where do you see yourself professionally in three to five years?"

Second, if advancement opportunities within the firm are slim, Lauren's desired job attributes may pose a barrier to her receiving the job offer. Likewise, if the firm sees career success and a private life as internal contradictions, Gabrielle is less likely to be offered the job. **That's not necessarily a bad thing.** Sometimes a firm can save you from a miserable career move by seeing that your values and the firm's expectations don't mesh.

Hints: 1. Be able to define in your own terms the meaning of each attribute. For example: What does Lauren mean by "Challenging Work?"

2. Know **why** that attribute is important to you. This will prepare you for any follow-up questions.

3. Think about how the most important attributes for you exist in the job for which you are interviewing.

Ace #77: Where Would You Like to Be Professionally in Three to Five Years?

This question is designed to get a sense of your professional aspirations, (hopefully, you have some) and to see how well they fit with what that company has to offer. Your response should show some desire for advancement, based on your performance and contributions to the firm.

Q. "George, you have explained your interest in the job we are discussing today. Where do you see yourself in three to five years?"

A. "You mentioned that this firm both demands and rewards outstanding performance. Within five years, I hope that I have demonstrated through my results that I should be moving towards regional manager."

Doing it Badly

If the question is about your professional goals, you can hurt yourself in any of three ways: Having no desire to move ahead; having ambitions which are unrealistic at least in the context of that firm; seeing no connection between performance and advancement.

A. "This is the job of my dreams. I can see being happy doing just this five, or even ten years from now."

Or

A. I see myself as a fast-track performer. Within three years I expect to have a job at your level, and by the end of five years I expect to be a senior vice president.

Or

A. I notice that some people have been promoted quickly here. That's what I expect.

Ace #78: Preparing for Your Goals

It's nice to have goals, and you will probably be asked about yours. A reasonable follow-up question would ask how you have prepared to achieve your immediate goal, namely a new job. This question probes how realistically you connect preparation with aspiration.

Q. "John, you mentioned your interest in becoming a

plant manager, similar to the position we have open here. How have you prepared yourself to reach that goal?"

Your answer should indicate the steps you have taken to gain the necessary experience for your next career move. As an example, John might give an answer like this:

A. "A good plant manager in this industry needs to combine several talents, namely technical knowledge, planning, interpersonal skills, and communication. Because of my engineering education, I had good technical skills even before I came to Presentco. It was during my second year in production planning that I started thinking about being a plant manager down the road. To sharpen my interpersonal skills, I made a point of volunteering for team assignments and cross-functional projects. I developed my oral communication by giving plant tours to college students in addition to planning presentations I made as part of my job."

This question invites you to show that the job for which you are interviewing is consistent with a deliberate process on your part, rather than just a target of opportunity.

Ace #79: Salary Expectations

One reason people go to work is to get paid. From the employer's point of view, asking about your salary expectations makes sense for two reasons. First, to see if your expectations are reasonable from the firm's perspective and second to check on their competitiveness in the hiring market. From your point of view, it is better **not** to answer the question. One reason is that any figure you give may be too high (e.g. unreasonable) or too low (e.g. low self esteem; not the right caliber). Second, the whole topic of compensation is best left until the job is offered to you. Some people undercut their potential salary by mentioning a low figure in the hope of not pricing themselves out of a job. Until the job is offered, you have no negotiating power to raise your salary. (For ways to ace your salary negotiations at the appropriate time, see Chapter 8). What you want is to defer the whole subject gracefully.

Q. "Jerry, give me a sense of what you would expect to be making if you came to work with us."

A. "I am sure that your compensation package is competitive and that we will be able to reach an agreement if you offer me this position."

It is possible that the interviewer will want to press for a more specific answer. In that case, you could have two possible fallback positions.

Q. "Well, we think that we are quite competitive, Jerry, but I would like to hear about the salary you would anticipate."

A. "My first priority is making sure that this job, if offered, is right for me. In terms of salary, it depends on the entire package. When the salary review would be, things like that. Overall, I would say that I am looking for mid $40s to low $50s."

In this answer Jerry has given a **range,** rather than a specific number. It is an answer which mitigates the too high/too low problem and leaves room for future negotiation.

If Jerry prefers not to state even a range, or if the above

response is followed by yet another question about salary, Jerry could say this:

A. "What are you planning to offer your finalists for this position?"

If Jerry responds in this way he must be careful to use an inquiring rather than an arrogant tone of voice.

Interviewing for a Sales Position

If you are interviewing for a position in sales, the topic of compensation needs to be addressed a bit differently.

In a sales career, making money (as in big bucks) is a major motivation. The person interviewing you will look for a strong indication that the potential for earning a large income is important to you. If you are asked in a sales interview, "How much money do you expect to make?" give a response like this: "It's difficult to say how much I might earn in the first year. However, by my third year, I expect to be making at least $50,000." (You can even add, "Do your top achievers earn that much by their third year?")

A desire to make money in a sales career is more than important—it is a prerequisite for getting hired. If your prospective employer stresses building long term relationships, rather than transactional sales, you could preface your response by saying: "Money isn't my only professional consideration, but it is one of them."

Ace #80: Contacting Employer & References

You may be asked a question like this:

Q. "May I contact your current employer and your references?"

The general tone of your response could be in the "yes, when" category.

A. "My references are aware that I am looking for a new position. When you have narrowed your field of candidates to the finalists, I am sure that they would welcome your call.

"In terms of my current employer, he and I have not yet discussed my job search. When you have decided that you are about to offer me the job, you could certainly contact him. However, please let me know beforehand so that he will hear about my move from me first."

There are several reasons for this response. Your references **should be** aware that they might be called by a prospective employer about your job search. You should have cleared that with each reference before using his/her name. Therefore, they won't be totally surprised if contacted.

Your employer is another matter. You may be jeopardizing your current position if s/he discovers your efforts to find a different job. If that might be your case, you need to be cautious. Don't allow a prospective employer to call your current boss unless the new offer is yours, pending that final step. Besides, professional courtesy and your interest in not burning bridges both suggest that you be the first one to break your plans to your boss.

Where Are We Now

In this chapter we looked at forty common historical questions and how to answer them. In the next chapter we will examine ten common behavioral questions.

Exercise 1: Preparing with "How" & "Why"

Noah Prepares for an Interview

One good way to prepare for an interview is to have a friend ask you "how" and "why" questions based on your

Doing it Badly

Here are some self destructive answers to questions we discussed in this chapter. Let's hope that you never give responses like these which were shared with me by human resource professionals:

Q."How do you deal with stress; how do you keep things under control when work gets hectic?"

A. "Full body massage and facial once a week; running every day."

Your response should focus on how you handle stress while still at work. Outside of work relaxation should be secondary if you include it at all.

Q. "What are your career goals over the next 3-5 years?"

A. "I don't have any, but don't worry. I'm sure I would burn out at this job long before then."

Usually, if you have no goals in the mid term or long run, you won't get the job at all.

Q. (To an accounting position applicant) "What were your duties and responsibilities in your last job?"

A. "Well, I worked with numbers." This response does not describe an accountant. If the previous job was not accounting related he should explain what professional skills he used that would help him be good in an accounting position.

Q. "Do you have the ability to maintain a confidence?"

A. Applicant said, "Yes," and then proceeded to tell all the details of an unpleasant incident, including the names of the individuals involved.

Your very behavior at the interview can undermine the answers you give.

Q. "Why do you want to work for us (from a retail company)?"

A. "I love to shop."

Nice, but no cigar. If the applicant had proceeded to tell how her shopping led to a professional interest, that would make sense.

Q. "Why do you want to work here?"

A. "I am longing for a secure job (firm had just gone through a well publicized downsizing)."

resume. "How" and "why" questions encourage you to think about yourself in terms of your approach to situations, the skills you use, and your motivation for doing whatever you did. Here is an example based on "Noah's Resume" on page 106. It also includes an example of the "question—answer—question" cycle, namely the interviewer drawing his/her next question from your previous answer.

Dove: "Noah, you indicate on your resume that you led the rescue of human and animal life from the Great Flood." That's quite impressive! Please tell me how you did that.

Noah: (Pauses a moment to collect his thoughts.) "It was a great undertaking, but I broke the problem into smaller segments to make them easier to solve. In this case, I assessed the probability of a flood at 100% since I heard about it from a Reliable Source. That left two main tasks: building the ark and gathering pairs of animals. Realizing that the tasks could be staffed simultaneously, I organized my sons and daughters-in-law into two total quality management teams. I explained to each team how vital their efforts would be. I coached and encouraged each team on a continuous basis. The results: When the first drop of rain fell, we were able to load a full menagerie of animals into a seaworthy ark."

Dove: "Why did you assign some individuals to one team and some to another?" (Note that Dove has taken a part of the previous answer as a basis for his next question.)

Noah: "You have to know your people. Shem and Ham get along well together and have good sense about animals. Yaphet is good with his hands and knows how to work through progressive stages with a picture of the final product clearly in mind."

Dove: "In your summary you say that you seek 'to build a career in selling insurance.' How did you arrive at that goal and why are you interested in **selling** insurance? Perhaps you could be an underwriter instead."

Noah: (Pauses a moment.) "The two parts of your question are connected. My interest in insurance developed from the trauma of The Flood. I realized that people need to be protected against the consequences of unforeseen catastrophes and insurance is one way to do that. Unfortunately many people don't think about insurance until it's too late. They need to be sold on the idea and that's what I want to do."

Dove: "Why do you think people will be interested in discussing floods with you now? Nobody outside of your family boarded your Ark before the Flood."

Noah: (Pauses) "That's a good point, but circumstances were very different. For one thing, my assigned task was to build the Ark and get pairs of animals to enter it. Persuading people outside my family to come aboard was not an objective. Second, the Flood itself is an object-lesson in the dangers of deluge. Today, people would be more concerned."

This brief excerpt from the Dove/Noah dialogue shows you how Noah gained practice in presenting his positive characteristics through easy to ask "how" and "why" questions. This process could be repeated for each line of the résumé, including "education." ("Noah, why did you decide to attend the School of Hard Knocks?")

Noah
Ararat Drive
Ancient City, World 10001
(333) 444-5678

Summary: Proven skills in leadership, communication, and problem solving. Demonstrated ability to assess risk and respond appropriately. Professional experience with The Flood and reconstruction. Seeks to build a career in selling insurance, with a special interest in flood insurance. Interest developed as a result of leading role played in worst flood in recorded history.

Work
Experience: *Flood Beater*
Led rescue of human and animal life from the Great Flood. Directed reestablishment of human life on earth. Assessed risk of destruction based on heavenly insight and gathering rain clouds. Responded by organizing thousands of creatures to board a custom-made ark in an orderly manner.

Solved both logistic and staff problems while completing ark under tight deadline. Communicated directly with ark passengers, thus minimizing discord during forty rough days at sea. Learned how to manage massive enterprise with minimal resources.

Carpenter
Built structures ranging from book shelves to family houses. Designed ark decks and accommodations for selected clients.

Education: *School of Hard Knocks*
Bachelor of Biblical Administration
Major: Management

Honors: "Righteous Man in His Generation" awarded in recognition of high moral character and trust of contemporaries.

Leadership
Activities: Chairman, Dove/Raven Contest; Vice President, Ararat 4-H Society

6

Ace the
Behavioral Interview

In recent years, the behavioral interview question has become more common. Reduced to its essentials, the behavioral question asks the interviewee to describe how s/he exhibited a particular "behavior," let's say a skill or attribute, in a recent situation. The firm has identified certain behaviors which seem to characterize successful people in that company. Therefore, it makes sense to ask the interviewee specifically about those behaviors rather than trying to infer them from answers to historical questions. Some advocates of behavioral questions also believe that they make the interview more objective and easier to validate in legal terms.

There are some **advantages** for you in the behavioral question.

- The point of the question is crystal clear.

- Based on your research of the job and the company, you should be able to identify many of the questions you will be asked.

- Your recent behavior, rather than possible historical weaknesses, is the topic. This is particularly
useful if you are transitioning to a new career or
industry.

- Potential objections are more likely to be raised,
rather than left unspoken (see chapter 4).

Of course, there are also some potential **disadvantages:**

- An inappropriate or missing behavior will become
more apparent.

- You may be more comfortable describing yourself
in terms of history or accomplishments.

- An interview comprising only behavioral questions
would tend to be more structured and less spontaneous. Therefore, you have less influence on
setting the agenda.

It is in the nature of the behavioral question to request
an answer **with examples.** I recommend drawing your
examples from more than one source so you don't sound
like a one-dimensional person. If you have a choice, work
related examples are usually better than those drawn from
your private life.

Some characteristics will display themselves in the
course of the interview even if you are never asked about
them. For example, enthusiasm shows through your
demeanor and preparation shows by your knowledge of
the company. Listening skills are demonstrated by how
closely your answers relate to the questions asked. Oral
communication is on exhibit throughout the interview.

Let's look at ten common topics for behavioral questions and how to ace them.

Ace #81: Leadership

Q.   "Judy, give me an example of how you exercised leadership in a recent situation."

Judy needs to provide an example **from her real life**. She does not need to be a CEO or Commander-in-Chief of the armed forces. Given that context, Judy could give an answer like this:

A.   "Just last week I completed an assignment on a team representing four different functions in the firm. No one had the title 'Team Leader,' but I showed leadership by keeping the team focused on the task. I also identified common ground solutions so we could make our policy recommendations with everyone on board."

In this response, Judy gave an example of leadership even though it was not a formal part of her title. The interviewer may follow-up by asking Judy **how** she kept the team focused or **why** the other members of the team accepted her leadership role.

If Judy doesn't have a leadership example, *per se*, she could start by saying: "I have never been in a leadership role as such, but I am a good team player who quickly wins respect from peers and co-operation from the necessary people. Let me give you an example."

Ace #82: Problem Solving

One skill which is in demand almost universally is problem solving:

Doing It Badly

Judy could hurt herself by picking a weak example of leadership like these:

A. "Whenever Mark and I work on a joint project, he tends to defer to my judgement."

This answer describes Mark's deference, not Judy's leadership. In addition, the response suggests a work world of only two people.

Or

A. "Whenever we go bowling, I'm the one who decides where to go for beer afterwards." The context makes this answer unconvincing.

Q.   "Beth, describe a recent problem and how you solved it."

This question is a bit like a figure skating competition. There, your score depends both on the complexity of your program and how well you execute it. Beth should try to describe a problem which the interviewer can relate to the job under discussion and which shows significant talent.

A.   "At Nowco, we had a problem with a client who gave us 10% of our business and 60% of our troubles. Some people thought we should drop the account, but I felt that one-tenth of our business was worth preserving. Instead of criticizing our client for ineptitude, I arranged a meeting with the announced purpose of identifying ways to serve them better. As a result, we ironed out some nettlesome communication problems, and booked some extra orders besides!"

This answer shows Beth taking a positive approach to a problem rather than the less aggravating approach of cutting bait. **Hint:** The revenue the account brought in could be quantified and tends to make the owner or manager happy. The trouble the client caused would be a more subjective matter. Besides, the aggravation might be yours, not theirs. Business seldom rewards losing revenue for the firm to save you aggravation, so Beth behaved wisely.

The question could have a different slant.

> Q. "Beth, tell me about a time when you were held accountable for a problem but you hadn't caused it."

Beth took a positive approach to avoid the danger of bad-mouthing someone.

> A. "I suppose there are going to be times when you could get involved in a 'who struck John?' scenario. The important thing is solving problems, not finding someone to blame. For example, last week we had a computer shut down. I focused on how to get it running again instead of looking for someone to point a finger at."

Ace #83: Dealing with Change

Change is becoming a constant in professional life. Technology, competition, management philosophies, law, a new generation of workers, all bring change. Often we can anticipate change, sometimes we can influence it, but we cannot avoid it. Therefore, it makes sense to ask how you deal with change.

> Q. "Marilyn, you must have seen some interesting developments in the five years you were at Nowco. Think about the changes you have seen and tell me how you handle change."

Marilyn realizes that she has indeed seen many changes.

Since she wants to keep her answer appropriately focused, she picks one change that will demonstrate at least one of Marilyn's positive characteristics.

A.   "Yes, I have seen a number of changes. I mentioned earlier some changes I caused. Let me tell you about one that I had to accommodate. We outsourced our sales function by contracting with a distributor. Feedback from our own salespeople had been an important source of information for me. To makeup for that loss, I established what ties I could to the distributor and also got more involved in asking for feedback from our customers."

Marilyn is showing by her response that she dealt constructively with the new reality she faced, even though she was not necessarily happy with the change that caused it.

Ace #84: Decision Making

As American business restructures, more decisions are being made by employees immediately involved with the situation, rather than passing the issue to a higher level. Therefore, a question about your decision making process would be reasonable irrespective of the position for which you are interviewing.

Q.   "Allan, tell me about a decision you made recently and how you reached it."

Allan has probably made a number of decisions recently. He wants to choose a situation that will allow him to show at least one positive characteristic. In that connection, Allan should plan on discussing a situation where there was something substantial at stake and the outcome was positive. It would also help Allan if the example he gives is similar to a situation which might arise at the prospective employer's. In this example, Allan is interviewing for a situation where client satisfaction is critical.

A.   "Of course, making decisions is a part of everyday work life. I have established a set of guiding principles and priorities and operate within that framework. Sometimes it gets a bit dicey. For example, our finance operation requested a production report. Normally, that kind of data is available at the end of each month. I would have had to re-assign someone from another project to get the report to finance two weeks earlier. I decided that keeping good relations with finance was worth the cost of the re-assignment, so we produced what they needed two weeks ahead of the normal schedule."

Allan might expect a follow-up question like: "Why didn't you stick to your guns and hold to the regular schedule?"

Or

"How did you explain to the re-assigned person the reason for the change?"

Or

"Did your decision cause any problems among your production staff?"

Ace #85: Criticism

Somerset Maugham said "People ask you for criticism but they want only praise." That may be true of the human condition, but it is not a very constructive approach in the work place. How do you handle a question like this?

Q. "Mindy, tell me about a time when you were criticized. What was the issue involved, who made the criticism and how did you handle it?"

Mindy needs to keep several points in mind while formulating her answer.

- She doesn't want to reveal any festering weaknesses.

- She shouldn't blame the critic.

- She is probably not the rare human being who has never been criticized or the equally rare person who enjoys criticism.

- She should learn something from the criticism she received.

With those thoughts in mind, Mindy gave an answer like this:

A. "I think it is important to be open to criticism. We want to provide an excellent service, and that requires honest input from both co-workers and outside clients. Recently, I was criticized by a marketing manager for making a presentation that got too detailed too early. I learned from that to think more like a marketer when making a presentation to a client and less like the technical person I was trained to be."

Ace #86: Communication Skills

It's not unlikely that you will hear a question like this one:

Q. "Dahlia, tell me how you use your communication skills, written and oral."

You don't have to be either Shakespeare or Demosthenes to address this question. In most cases, the prosaic, utilitarian use of language is what works best in the work place. This question requires a response addressing both forms of communication. In this response, Dahlia starts with her stronger skill.

A. "I have effective communication skills. For example, I give frequent presentations to both clients and senior management. Both have told me that my oral presentations are effective. For example, last week a client told me that it was my presentation which persuaded his firm to place a large order with us.

"I also write clearly and concisely. Most of my writing is on day-to-day subjects. My goal is to get the information transmitted completely and accurately. I don't do a lot of drafting and editing with e-mail. When it comes to progress reports, however, I carefully consider what my boss wants to know. Last month's report was typical. I did several drafts to make sure the report was accurate, concise and inclusive."

Ace #87: Time Management

Time is money and both are under tight constraints. Successful people tend to be good time managers, so a question like this is common:

Q. "Think about a recent project you were assigned. How did you go about managing your time and organizing the project."

This is a two part question, so address both parts.

A. "A recent project I was assigned involved gathering information for an SEC filing. The difficulty was in getting the right pieces from the right people on time. I arranged a chart showing what I needed and when, with estimated lead times. The shorter the lead time, the higher on my priority list that contact had to be. Since we have offices on both coasts, I arranged to call the California operations late in the day by east coast time.

"Of course this wasn't my only responsibility. I deferred doing some longer range or less pressing projects. Then I gave this project three hours a day, and completed my other responsibilities during the rest of the day."

Ace #88: Teamwork

Since team work is a common approach to getting things done (often faster, better and less expensively) your skills in this area are likely to be probed. Expect a question like this one:

Q. "Judy, team work is critical to our success at

Thisco. Please tell me about a recent team you worked on."

Let's assume that Judy has already discussed one team project in response to a question about leadership. It would be better for Judy to choose another example this time.

A. "A few months ago, all five marketing people formed a team to evaluate our performance over the past year as a basis for planning for next year. One thing I contributed was reaching an agreement that we would report as a team. That way we avoided defensiveness or any tendency to point fingers."

What Judy has done here is indicate a major contribution to the team's success that would be important to a prospective employer as well. She did not discuss what the team reported since that would be proprietary information.

Doing It Badly

Making a team productive is difficult and even one player with the wrong attitude could make it more so. Luckily, Judy did not give an answer like this:

A: "One thing I'm good at is making sure that everybody pulls their weight. For example, we had a fellow from another department who just didn't take things seriously. Everything was 'later' or 'we'll see' or 'not yet.' Finally, I got tired of it and complained to his boss."

This sounds like the "I'm going to tell the teacher on you" approach. Professionals on a team should at least try to solve problems like the one described **internally**. A response like: "I sat down and discussed with this person how important his participation was and that we were all depending on him," would have been more appropriate.

Ace #89: Persuasion

You may be asked to describe how you use your skills of persuasion. Remember, communication conveys information, persuasion impacts on the other person's actions.

Q. "Jeanneane, have you ever had to persuade someone to do something they were initially reluctant about?"

Hints: Don't answer this question with a one word answer like "yes." The intent is to have you **describe** the situation. Also, your example should show the **process** of persuasion and not just the outcome.

A. "Persuasion is a common part of my work life. For example, I may need to persuade the accounting people to give me some data before their quarterly report is due. Or, last month I needed to persuade a committee to authorize an agreement with one outsourcing firm rather than another. I do this in two ways. First, I have consciously built a reputation as a reasonable and fair person who wouldn't try to put one over on anybody. Second, I ask questions to determine why the other party is reluctant to support my preferences or determined to promote their own. I have been successful in showing people how my preference actually meets their needs."

Ben was faced with a similar question:

Q. "Ben, tell me how you persuade people to accept your point of view."

Ben remembered some of the keys to persuasion. Listening to and respecting others; speaking in terms of the other person's interest or a common interest, and not just your own. With that in mind, Ben responded like this:

A. "I have been a member of several cross-functional teams this year. One of my goals is to listen carefully to what the finance and marketing people are concerned about and not just hammer away at engineering's point of view. The team's goal through co-operation is to make sound decisions that minimize costly mistakes like redesigning a product after it has been brought to market. So I did some reading about capital constraints and price-points to better understand the business concerns. That has earned me the respect of the finance and marketing people. It also enabled me to present engineering's point of view in ways that address their concerns. That has helped engineering get business function support for more of its projects."

Ben has indicated that he is persuasive because he listens, understands and speaks to the concerns of others. He did not claim to be 100% successful all the time. That's reasonable, particularity in light of the team's goal, which is to promote the objectives of the company as a whole, and not just one functional area.

Ace #90: Pressure

There are all kinds of pressures in the professional world and each of us has to find a way of dealing with it. Rose may hear a question like this:

Q. "Tell me about a time when you were under enormous pressure. What was the source of the pressure and what did you do?"

A. "Pressure is a constant because I have to deal with getting the most value added under conflicting demands. The pressure gets worse during quarterly closings because we want to book the largest amount of orders without throwing our production schedule out of kilter.

"I deal with the pressure in two ways. One is that I don't add to it by constantly second guessing myself. I establish a game plan and stick with it. The other is that, on my own time, I jog and do yoga to relax."

Rose wisely chose an example that demonstrates a situation with some connection to her prospective employer. In this case, it was conflicting demands. This is something the interviewer can relate to his own firm's situation even if they don't have a production schedule as such. Rose also based her response primarily on her business context, and mentioned outside of work relaxation secondarily.

Where Are We Now?

In this chapter we looked at ten behavioral questions and how to ace them. In the next chapter we will look at an often neglected subject that can be as important as your answers: Questions you should ask the interviewer.

7

Asking Good Questions

In the last two chapters, we looked at different questions
you might be asked and how to answer them. In this
chapter, we will discuss a subject which can be just as
important to your interview success but is often overlooked:
Questions **you should ask** at your interview.

Ace #91: Understanding Why
Your Questions Are Critical

Here are four reasons why your questions to the interviewer are critical:

- Your questions may be as important as your answers when the interviewer evaluates you. This is
  because your questions reveal a lot about you, for
  example: your interests and priorities; your degree
  of preparation; your energy and communication
  skills; your ability to relate general situations to that
  firm's particular reality.

- The questions you ask at the end of your interview are totally within your control. You set the agenda by the questions you ask. To make an analogy to a test, you are in charge of about half the points needed to score 100! Similarly, the more spontaneous questions you could ask in the midst of your interview are **almost** totally within your control.

- The **answers** you get may help you with further stages of the interview process since they increase your understanding of the job, the company and the industry.

- The answers may help you in **evaluating** a job offer, if you receive one.

5 Rules to Ace Your Questions

Almost all interviewers will solicit your questions, usually 5-10 minutes before the end of the interview. There are **5** basic rules to remember about asking good questions.

Ace #92: You Care

If you don't care don't ask. Why jeopardize the interviewer's confidence in your sincerity? Caring also means that your purpose in asking is not to stump the interviewer.

For example: Shirley could ask about the profitability of the firm's widget division. "I read in **Widget Weekly** that growth in this product line has been slow for the past two years. Do you think that corporate headquarters will be patient enough to stick with widgets until they become as profitable as gizmos?"

Because Shirley really cares, she is perceived as sincere and would be ready for a follow-up question like "Why is the profitability of our widget line of particular interest to you?"

If Shirley had asked "Why is line 37 of your 10K so low?" she would likely be perceived as trying to play Stump the Interviewer. That's a losing game.

Ace #93: Your Question Reflects Prior Research and Thought

Your question should build upon subjects you have already read about and thought about. Further, your question should **reflect** that research and thought. For example: "I read in Yourco's annual report that Mr. Jefferson, the chairman, anticipates intensified competition from emerging firms in the industry. Will this department be involved in fostering the improved client services that Mr. Jefferson envisions as a response?"

Remember that an interview is a business meeting. Would you go to a business meeting, let's say with a customer, without doing some preliminary research? In addition to **doing** your research, reflect it in your question. If you had simply asked, "Will this department be involved in fostering improved client services?" it wouldn't be nearly as helpful to you.

Questions which follow this rule reflect well on your preparation, seriousness and insight.

Ace #94: Avoid Raising Needless Barriers

Few people enjoy being asked about their weaknesses. Unfortunately, some people imply they have a weakness by the way they ask a question. For example: "Would there be a lot of travel involved with this job?"

This question implies that you might have a problem with travel. That certainly won't help you but it may be a barrier to getting the offer—especially if travel is involved. If you

---

Doing It Badly

Don't let your question indicate a lack of research by asking a question like this:

"Where does senior management think competition will come from in the future?"

You shouldn't enter the interview room completely unaware of the firm's competition.

Avoid an overly generic question that reflects no prior thought at all:

"Everyone is concerned about being competitive. How does this firm stay competitive?"

---

are lucky, the interviewer will follow-up to clarify any doubts that have been raised. If you are unlucky, the implied barrier will be there but the job offer won't.

The better way of asking about travel is this: "I know that many jobs involve overnight travel and that is not a problem for me. However, I would like to know what the mix of travel and in-office assignments might be."

Stated this way, you are showing an interest in the pragmatics of the job without raising any avoidable doubts.

Ace #95: Ask the Appropriate Person

Is the person receiving your question appropriate based on his/her standing in the firm and the issues s/he deals with on a professional basis?

For example, if you are speaking with someone who has recently joined the firm, questions about his/her transition and his/her experiences in the new job make sense. If the individual holds a job much like the one you are seeking, lots of questions about the job, reporting relationships, and resources, objectives are appropriate.

Doing It Badly

Some people put barriers to potential jobs in their own paths by asking poor questions like these:

Q. "Do you offer flextime arrangements for people like me who are committed to daily exercise?"

(Barriers: "Can you be at work when we need you? What are your priorities?")

Or

Q. "Your affirmative action policy won't hold me back, would it?"

(Barriers: "Do you have an attitude problem in regard to ethnic minorities or women?")

Or

Q. "Is office romance forbidden here?"

(Barriers: "Are you a sexual harassment suit waiting to happen? What are your real motives for wanting this job?")

Or

Q. "What are your psychiatric benefits?"

(Barriers: "Does this person understand about the appropriate time to ask questions? Does this person have personal problems that will interfere with job performance?")

On the other hand, a different set of questions makes sense for senior managers. Your questions might more reasonably focus on firm strategy, pressing issues, future challenges and his/her process for evaluating the staff.

If the interviewer is a line manager from a different function, be sure to ask questions about their responsibilities and how their function and yours would work together.

Ace #96: Be Prepared for Reasonable Counter Questions

A good interviewer may ask a question as part of his/her response to your question. For example: "Lauren, you asked about competitive challenges this firm will face in the future. One thing I mentioned in response is high quality imports from Singapore. Do you have any ideas about how we can meet this challenge?" (**Hint:** see Aces 2 and 25.

Or

"Michael, you asked about where you might be in this firm in three to five years. I gave you several possibilities. As we sit here today, which path seems most attractive to you? Why?" (**Hint:** See Ace 77.)

Or

"Gabrielle, I hope I answered your question. Why are you interested in this topic?" (**Hint:** see Ace 72.)

4 Topics for Building Your Questions

Constructing good questions may seem like a daunting task. You can make it more manageable by building questions around the following four topics.

Ace #97: The Job Itself

The single most important topic is the job itself. After all, your purpose at the interview is to show the prospective employer that you are a good (perhaps the best) candidate for the job. Keeping in mind the five rules we discussed in the previous section, you could ask questions like these:

Q. "I noticed from reading Yourco's annual report and some back press releases that your three most senior managers are engineers. Sometimes there must be differences of opinion between the finance and engineering departments. Do you have any problems getting a fair hearing for the finance point of view?"

Or

Q. "I am interested in knowing how much of a typical day is spent working on the computer and how much time is spent assisting customers."

Doing It Badly

Here are some awful questions some have people asked about the job that damaged their chances for employment.

"The job description mentions week-end work. Would I really have to do that?"
(Damage: This person really isn't available for weekend work.)

"The job title is _____. Who thought of that name?"
(Damage: This person focuses on the trivial.)

"How long do I have to wait before I get promoted?"
(Damage: This is an impatient, me-first candidate.)

"My real interest in this job is to get my foot in the door and then

---

Ace #98: The Company

Sometimes prospective brides are reminded that they not just marrying the groom, they also marrying the in-laws. A similar situation prevails in your career. Jobs don't exist in a vacuum. You will be working in an organization called a firm, a company or something similar. How that company operates and how it sees itself will have a major influence on your work life and your career. You could ask questions like these:

Q. "Your annual reports indicate that revenues have grown at an annual rate of 14% for 3 years. Do you think that this rate can be sustained as the firm grows larger?"

Or

Q. "Setting realistic goals can be difficult. Does Yourco have any formal process for establishing goals by benchmarking against a competitor's performance?"

Or

Q. "All the people I have spoken with at this firm seem to be proud of working here. What is it about this company which instills such pride?"

Doing It Badly

Would you be favorably impressed by a job candidate who asked questions like these?:

"What does your company do, anyway?" (Shows lack of research)

"Who makes the big decisions here?" (Unprofessional tone: impatient; may not understand decision making process)

"Why does this firm emphasize team work so much? High flyers like me could get the job done ourselves!" (Lone Ranger complex; not a team player)

"You are getting some bad press over bribery and faulty products issues. Is anybody around here embarrassed by all that?" (Lacks tact)

Ace #99: The Industry

Just as jobs don't exist in a vacuum, neither do companies. You might want to ask a question like this regarding the industry of which your prospective new company is a part:

> Q. "A number of firms in the industry have merged in an effort to reduce costs. Do you think other firms may follow this path, or will they prefer the agility that being medium sized can provide?"

Doing It Badly

Think before you ask a question so you won't shoot yourself in the foot the way these people did:

"Yourco is number three in the industry. Do firms of this size have a future?" (This question does indicate knowledge of a fact, but it doesn't indicate that the job candidate has given the fact any further thought.

"Do you think mergers will result in more layoffs in this industry?" (This question suggests a sense of insecurity rather than any specific insight.)

"Who is going to be number one in this industry in a few years?" (Firms are more concerned with profits than prophecy. Besides, this question doesn't reflect anything positive about the job candidate.)

Ace #100: Outside Influences

There are events beyond the control of an industry, firm or individual which can have a major influence on all three. Legislation, trade treaties, natural phenomena are some examples. To show that you think broadly enough to consider the implications of outside influences, you could ask a question like this:

> Q. "There is a prediction for a shorter, milder winter this year. Can you tell me how this is impacting on

orders from retailers for the Warmwool Sweater line?"

Or

Q. "If Congress passes a one cent a pound levy on sugar, will there be any way of keeping the price of this firm's candy bars from rising?"

Or

Q. "According to new trade agreements, certain disputes will be referred to the World Trade Organization for adjudication. Will that impact Widgetco's export strategy?"

Ace #101: Closing—Winning by Doing it Right

Interviews, like all business meetings, are held to achieve a purpose. Your purpose at the interview is to get the job offer. By closing properly, you can advance your cause. Broadly speaking, ask for the job:

Peter: "I have enjoyed meeting with you today, Janice. Unfortunately our time is up. Thank you for coming in and interviewing with us."

Janice: "Thank you, Peter, I have enjoyed meeting with you as well. I am interested in this job. What's our next step?"

In all likelihood, Peter will give Janice a non-committal response like: "You'll be hearing from us soon." That's all right. The value of the question is in the asking. There are three ways.

More Examples of Questions You Could Ask

1. "When you are working with other functional areas, are you expected to represent this department's views or do you take the approach of a team member working for a common cause?"

2. "Can you please tell me how your career has developed at Happy Corp. and would someone entering the firm today have similar opportunities?" (**Hint:** Be prepared for the counter questions "Where would you like to be in five years?")

3. "I read that your training program is comprised of three, six month rotations. Does the employee have any input into where s/he will go at the end of each rotation? How do you evaluate the employee's performance during the training period?"

4. "I read in Business Week that a major competitor, Eager Corp., is increasing its market share in your main market. What plans does your firm have to regain its lost market share?" (**Hint:** Be prepared for the counter-question: "Do you have any suggestions for increasing our market share?")

5. "I am excited about the possibility of working for Super Corp., but I am also concerned about the turnover rate among your new hires. What accounts for the high turnover rate and are any steps being taken to correct this situation?" (Obviously, you only ask a question of this type if you are sure of your facts, i.e. there actually is a high turnover rate.)

6. "Some articles in the business press have speculated that consumers will be holding their wallets tighter because of a heavy personal debt load. Do you think that firms in this industry will engage in price cutting or develop less complicated products if that becomes the case?"

7. "If the federal government reduces Medicare outlays, will the market for your Home Health Care appliances increase or decrease?" (**Hint:** Be prepared for the counter-question: "As you follow the Medicare debate, what do you think the consequences to this firm might be?")

- **Remove Doubts.** It is important that the interviewer does not have doubts about your interest in the job. Doubt stands in the way of taking the hiring process to the next step.

- **Showing Business Sense.** You may feel that you just want to go home and relax after your interview. However, it is important to show you that you have the business sense to reach closure for some results.

- **Preparing Better**. It is uncomfortable to ask for the job. Many people will prepare better for their interview because that will make them feel more worthy of asking about the next step.

Special Note

If you are interviewing for a commission based job, such as sales, ask for the job in so many words:

"I want this job. Are you going to offer it to me?"

For a sales job, not asking for the job could be fatal. If you can't ask for the job, you won't ask for the order either.

Some Parting Thoughts About Your Questions

Here are some parting thoughts about asking questions at your job interview.

- **Asking without an invitation:** Some people feel comfortable asking the interviewer a question even before being invited to do so. The important things to remember are:

The first time ask, "Do you mind if I ask you a question?" If the interviewer says, "that's fine," proceed with your question. Make **sure you relate your question to the subject** you have been discussing. For example:

Hanna: "George, do you mind if I ask you a question?"

George: (Nodding his head) "Sure, go ahead."

Hanna: "We have been discussing my experience with computers. What particular software packages are used in Yourco's processing center?"

Suppose George had said "sure, go ahead," but appeared less than genuinely receptive. Hanna would have asked her one question and then waited for an invitation to ask any more.

Hanna should understand that George might say, "Let's hold your questions until the end of the interview."

- **Written Questions:** Some people benefit by writing out their questions completely before the interview, others prefer some notes or an outline. It is appropriate to refer to your written questions at the interview, if you ask for permission. You can say, "I wrote down a number of questions while doing my interview preparation. Do you mind if I refer to the notes I made?" The interviewer will probably raise no objections but many people feel more comfortable if they are asked before written material is suddenly drawn into the interview.
  Refer, don't read. You can refer to your notes to help you recall the subject and substance of your question, but try **not to read it** straight from the paper. You will be more credible and less mechanical that way.

Repeating Questions

If a question is important to you, you could ask it to more than one interviewer from the same firm. However, after the first time, preface your question with: "Earlier in the day I asked James Johnson about the role of gizmos at Yourco and I would appreciate hearing your perspective as well."

Something to Avoid

Some people discuss an issue extensively during the interview and then ask a question as though it were based on a brand new topic. Doing that makes it seem that you haven't been listening. The right approach is to say, "George, earlier in the interview we had a discussion about developing strategies to account for interest rate fluctuations. I would like to pursue that topic with a question."

Where Are We Now

In this chapter, we discussed a topic critical to your interview success: asking good qestions. We explained why your questions are so important and the rules for asking questions that will favorably impress your interviewer. We looked at building your questions around four key topics and provided examples of questions, both good and bad.

In the next chapter, we will look at some dynamite aces to follow-up your interview.

8

Dynamite Follow-up Steps

Ace #102: Make Complete Notes
About What Happened

A by-product of your interview is what you learn from it.
One way to do this is to sit in a quiet place as soon after
your interview as possible. Make complete notes about
what transpired. For example, what was the first question
and how did you answer? If there was a follow-up question
to any of your responses, what was it? Did any questions
make you uncomfortable and catch you unprepared? Also
make note of the answers to your questions and any steps
the interviewer suggested you make subsequent to your
interview.

The purpose of these notes is to strengthen your next
interview in three ways. First, the interviewer's questions,
both initial and follow-up, reflect issues of importance to
the prospective employer. You want to pay special attention to these in preparing for a second interview with the

same company or an interview with another firm in the same industry. Second, questions which made you uncomfortable also need to be examined. Were you uncomfortable because the subject hit a sore spot? Is this a subject which you can handle in a way which puts an awkward situation in the best light? Third, the interviewer's answers to your questions can help you frame better questions in the future. For example: "At my previous interview here, Grace Meals mentioned that Thisco has been able to make rapid adjustments to the market because you have a flat managerial structure. As Thisco grows, will it be possible to retain your current degree of flexibility?"

Ace #103: Thank You Note

The main reason to write a brief thank you note is that it is good business etiquette. In addition the note may help your candidacy especially if it alleviates doubts about your interest in the job.

These are the main points of your thank you note.

- Convey your thanks.

- Refer to a specific part of the interview which you feel worked to your benefit.

- Express your enthusiasm for the job.

- Allay an objection expressed by the interviewer if you have a strong case to present.

- Refer to a next step.

Here is a sample.

Thank You Note

1739 North Aberdeen Street
Milwaukee, WS 53208

February 2, 1997

Ms. Judith Retriever
Vice President Marketing
Nextco Industries
1745 Blizzard Drive
Green Bay, WS 53201

Dear Ms. Retriever,

It was a pleasure meeting with you on February 1. Our discussion was thought provoking and fruitful, as I hope you will agree. The ideas we explored about applying my experiences at Dyno-Soar to your new line of paleolithic toys were especially interesting.

As a result of our meeting, I am even more enthusiastic about the possibility of joining your marketing staff. I am certain that my experience in the packaged goods industry would add a new dimension to the excellent team you already have in place.

If you would like to follow up on anything we discussed at the interview, please give me a call. May I look forward to participating in the next round of the interview process?

Sincerely,

Rebecca Benly

Rebecca Benly

A few extra notes:

- I recommend using Mr. or Ms. when addressing a senior manager unless s/he explicitly asked to be called by his/her first name.

- If you want to allay an expressed objection, don't repeat the objection. Just state your strong point which will compensate for it. In the sample letter above, Rebecca linked her knowledge of dinosaurs and experience with packaged goods to Nextco's paleolithic line of toys. This is intended to offset Rebecca's lack of experience with toys.

Ace #104: Touch Base With Your Network

A number of people have been interested in the progress of your job search. Some of them have been helpful by giving you advice, encouragement or leads. It is a courtesy to keep them posted about important developments like an interview. While courtesy should be a sufficient motivation, there could be two pragmatic benefits as well.

First, people appreciate hearing from you when you are not asking for a favor. It's like adding water to the well instead of constantly dipping in with your bucket. Second, someone in your network may be prompted to take some extra step to help you, for example offering new advice or being an even stronger reference.

Ace #105: Maintain Contact

There is some disadvantage in being out of sight and therefore out of mind. The person who interviewed you may not place your job candidacy as high on his/her priority list as you would rank it on yours. Therefore, it is helpful to push your candidacy closer to the front burner by maintaining **an appropriate degree of** contact with the interviewer. A week or so after the interview, call and inquire about your status. You could say something like: "This is Roberta Johnson. I am following-up on the interview we had last week. Can you tell me if there have been any developments so far?" You will probably get a non-committal response, but that doesn't matter. The point in your favor is that you have the interest and drive to follow-up.

Another thing you can do is to look for items in the press which relate to the job, the firm or industry you discussed. Drop your interviewer a short letter relating the news item to your prospective new job. Here is an example:

Follow-up Letter

2126 Ponce Street
Philadelphia, PA 19152
March 6, 1996

Mr. Daniel Goodman
Dairy Products International
2536 Lindenwood Street
Bristol, PA 19076

Dear Dan,

I want to thank you again for the opportunity to interview with you a few weeks ago. Since that time, I have been delving deeper into potential new markets for dairy products. In that connection, I thought that the enclosed article from the Lactose Intolerant Benevolent Association's national newsletter may be of interest. The article suggests that some individuals who usually cannot consume dairy products might be able to eat provolone or muenster if they combine it with salsa. This potential new market may be worth exploring.

Needless to say, I remain interested in joining your marketing staff and identifying as yet untapped markets for Dairy Products International.

Sincerely,

Michael Wrest

Michael Wrest

While appropriate follow-up is a plus, be careful not to make yourself **a pest**. For example, if the interviewer says that a decision will be made in seven to ten days, don't call to inquire about your status until at least eight days have passed. After that, don't call more frequently than once a week. If the interviewer says "no phone calls, please," don't call at all. There is a line between being interested and being a pest. Don't cross it!

Doing It Badly

Here are some more ill considered ways to follow-up that interviewers shared with me based on their own experiences:

- Invite the interviewer to dinner.

- Call the interviewer at home to ask about your status.

- Send the interviewer a cake (for himself) and pigs feet (for his dog.)

- Threaten to "take my case straight to the Chairman."

A Word of Caution

Most of this chapter is devoted to follow-up taken at your own initiative. If you **are requested** to follow-up with forms, transcripts, recommendations, etc., make sure you do so within the time frame indicated to you. A late follow-up could cost you the job.

Ace #106: Keep Looking for New Job Prospects

After your interview, you have a right to feel good, especially if you handled your part of the interview well. But a good interview is not yet a good job offer. What's more, even if a job **is** offered, you have the right to say **no**. So it is in your best interest to continue sourcing leads and seeking interviews.

There are **three** benefits to you.

- Your next job may be one you haven't even interviewed for yet. Interviews are dates, not marriages. You have no reason to stay home and do nothing while waiting for a prospective employer to respond.

- You will be under less stress in terms of any specific firm if you know that other options are developing.

- Having more than one option puts you in a stronger negotiating position when it comes to discussing compensation.

Even having a good interview under your belt is not the time to take a break. It is a time to keep on running.

Ace #107: Follow-up Visit

Let's picture Michael visiting his mail box. Inside is a letter from Happyco, a firm for which Michael wants to work. With great excitement, Michael goes inside his home and reads the letter. It's a job offer from Happyco!

Hearing the sounds of mirth and gladness, Daniel, Michael's good neighbor, knocks on the door. "My job search is over," Michael shouts. "Not so fast," Daniel suggests.

Daniel suggests that Michael arrange to visit Happyco again. He has three reasons:

- It will give Michael a chance to see Happyco when he is not under the stress of interviewing. That will give Michael a chance to see and feel things he may have missed during his interviews. Besides, Happyco will be less likely to be putting on a special, happy face for Michael during his follow-up visit.

- The follow-up visit may influence Michael's decision. He may experience negatives which weigh against accepting the offer or positives which will make Michael even more enthusiastic. Either way, the follow-up visit will add to Michael's peace of mind by helping him have the best and most complete sense of the situation at Happyco before responding to their offer.

- A third advantage is this: Michael is more likely to be successful in negotiating for more (let's say more money) if he is sure that he wants the job and he negotiates face to face.

Negotiating for more is the subject of Ace #108 & #109.

Ace #108: The Ethical Stall

Vicky is between jobs and she has a dilemma. She has interviewed with both Goodco and Topchoice, Inc. Goodco has offered Vicky a position and set April 15 as a deadline for Vicky's decision. Her first day of work would be May 7. But Vicky is really more interested in Topchoice, which has promised to let her know, one way or the other, by April 25.

What should Vicky do? One friend advised Vicky to accept the job at Goodco, "to make sure you're not left without a job." If Topchoice also extends an offer "accept that one, too," her friend advised. "Then, call Goodco, apologize and tell them you changed your mind," the friend concluded.

Vicky was troubled by this advice, and rightly so. Accepting an offer of employment while remaining open to something better is the ethical equivalent of accepting an offer of marriage, while remaining open to someone better. In this case, it would mean disrupting the hiring plans of Goodco and perhaps preventing someone else from getting that job. On a more pragmatic basis, Vicky was also concerned about damage to her professional reputation.

Vicky decided to do the ethical thing. First, she called Goodco and asked for an extension on the deadline date. Vicky based her request simply on needing a little more time to decide. "This is an important decision and I want to make sure I have thought it through completely," she said. Goodco extended the deadline one week to April 22. Vicky realized that she had nothing to lose by asking since the firm wouldn't withdraw the offer simply because she requested an extension.

"Progress, but not a solution yet," thought Vicky. So she called Topchoice and said "I wanted you to know that I remain very interested in Topchoice. In fact, working for you would be my first preference. However, I am in a difficult situation. Another firm has offered me a position and absolutely needs to hear from me by April 22. If you are going to offer me a position, I hope you can let me know by April 21."

If Topchoice, Inc. lets Vicky know its decision by April 21, her timing problem is over. She doesn't need to respond to Goodco before knowing all her options. (However, in this scenario Vicky won't have the time to schedule a follow-up visit the way Michael did.)

If Topchoice cannot make its decision before April 21, Vicky needs to decide yes or no on Goodco. She has to remember that "yes means yes" and **not** "yes, unless I get a better offer."

Negotiating for More

Your main purpose in the interview process is to secure a good job offer. One of the things that makes an offer good is how well you will be compensated. As a general rule, more is better than less when it comes to getting paid for any particular job. This section will discuss three steps you should take to increase your compensation package. Usually that means salary, but for you it may include other considerations such as starting date, staff support or bonus provisions.

Ace #109: Ask for More

Your interview process hasn't really been a total success unless you are given a job offer which makes you happy. If the substance of the job itself seems appealing, then I would negotiate for more compensation. There are two reasons to ask for more.

- **You Might Get It.** More money is better than less. Since in some jobs, bonuses and next year's salary are based on your current salary, the size of your starting salary may impact on your future salary as well.

- **Peace of Mind.** Let's assume that your negotiations don't produce an extra dollar. At least you will avoid the nagging doubt about how much you could have gotten had you only tried. Nagging doubts are bad for your morale.

Let's look at the "how" of negotiating now that we have looked at the "why." You are in a strong negotiating position if you can honestly make a statement like this. "I want this job. I like the job, the company and the people I would be working with. Only one thing is making me hesitate about saying yes, and that's the salary (or bonus provisions, etc). If you could increase the salary offer to $_____(name the amount), I would say 'yes' right away." A statement like this tells the prospective employer exactly what it would take to reach an immediate agreement. Since there is often upward flexibility on the employer's part you may get all, or at least some, of the increased salary you are seeking.

It is important to ask in the right way. Let's say John is asking for his salary offer to be increased from $60,000 to $65,000. He politely indicates hesitation, **not a counter offer**. For example, John **doesn't** say "I will accept your offer only if you increase my salary to $65,000."

Similarly, don't back yourself into a corner. John has maneuver room to accept the offer at less than $65,000 if he follows the advice given here. However, if John says, "The job just isn't worth it to me for less than $65,000" he has backed himself into a corner from which there is no graceful retreat.

One employment manager pointed out to me a partial exception to this ace. If the firm has stated clearly that the salary offer was the best they would make, there is little sense in pursuing that point. Instead you might try to negotiate an earlier salary review or a larger operating budget.

Ace #110: Pick the Right Time

You are more likely to get what you want if you negotiate face to face, preferably with a person who has the power to make a decision. The advantages of a face to face meeting are: it is harder to say no when you are looking directly at some one; in person meetings tend to be allocated more time than phone conversations.

You might state the purpose of meeting as wanting to clarify the offer. Rather than starting with a discussion of salary, review the nature of the job itself, reporting relationships, goal setting, etc. Assuming that you still want the job, now is the time to mention that you are enthusiastic but hesitant. If the firm could only raise the salary offer to, let's say, the high $60's you would say yes right away.

Ace #111: Be Prepared if the Answer is No

The previous two aces were designed to increase the probability of success in negotiating for a higher salary. However even the best negotiator is not always successful.

Before starting a negotiation, be clear in your own mind what you will do if the answer is no. There are several possibilities.

- **Leave the Door Open.** Express your disappointment. Then indicate that you will continue to think about the offer and respond by the firm's designated decision date.

I prefer this option for three reasons. First, it gives you time to test your feelings against the lower figure and perhaps reconcile to this reality. Second, silence and uncertainty are a bit nerve racking for everyone. Deferring a final response gives the prospective employer time to change his/her mind. Third, deferring gives you more time to clarify for yourself other options.

- **A Disappointed Yes.** Another option is to express your disappointment, but accept the offer anyway. You might decide on this approach because you need closure for professional or personal reasons. If you restate how much you want the job and indicate that you understand the firm's limitations in the matter, this approach may feel less awkward. Remember to be a happy camper when you accept the offer. Being a sourpuss is no way to start a new job.

From Lemons to Lemonade

No matter how well you do at your job interview, there is always a chance that you will not be offered the job. Since getting at least an occasional no is highly probable, let's look at some thing you can do to make the most of the situation.

Differently or Better

Call the person who interviewed you. Indicate that you know that the firm had many good candidates to choose from; that you are disappointed in not being the final candidate. Then say something like this: "Robert, I am still pursuing a new job in this field and your advice would be important to me. What could I have done differently or better?"

Even if Robert chooses to give you a hollow response, you have lost nothing by asking. On the other hand, Robert may decide to offer you some helpful feedback. For example, maybe it was a problem of substance like technical knowledge or experience in a certain industry. Perhaps it was a matter of style. Either way, you could consider changes as you continue your job search.

No and You

Think about your interview situation. What does the **no** say about you? If you are still interested in pursuing job opportunities of the same type perhaps you should increase your networking to identify more opportunities. If the **no** has so discouraged you that you want to stop looking, maybe you weren't that interested in the first place.

In any event, a rejection letter should be a statement that the company felt that another candidate was a better match than you. It is not a rejection of you as a person and you shouldn't see it as indicating that you'll never get another job.

I would love to hear from you about your own interview experiences. You can contact me at:

Richard Fein
University of Massachusetts
School of Management
Amherst, MA 01003
e-mail: rfein@som.umass.edu

Index

Career Resources

C ontact Impact Publications for a free annotated listing of career resources or visit their World Wide Web site for a complete listing of career resources: http://www.impactpublications.com.
The following career resources, many of which were mentioned in previous chapters, are available directly from Impact Publications. Complete the following form or list the titles, include postage (see formula at the end), enclose payment, and send your order to:

IMPACT PUBLICATIONS
9104-N Manassas Drive
Manassas Park, VA 20111-2366
Tel. 703/361-7300 or Fax 703/335-9486
E-mail address: impactp@impactpublications.com

Orders from individuals must be prepaid by check, moneyorder, Visa, MasterCard, or American Express. We accept telephone and fax orders.

Qty.	TITLES	Price	TOTAL
____	111 Dynamite Ways to Ace Your Job Interview	13.95	_____

Key Directories/Reference Works

Qty.	TITLES	Price	TOTAL
____	500 Largest U.S. Corporations	14.95	_____
____	American Almanac of Jobs and Salaries	20.00	_____
____	American Salaries & Wages Survey	105.00	_____
____	Big Book of Minority Opportunities	39.95	_____
____	Big Book of Opportunities For Women	39.95	_____
____	Business Phone Book USA 1997	135.00	_____
____	Careers Encyclopedia	39.95	_____
____	Complete Directory For People With Disabilities	149.95	_____
____	*Complete* Guide For Occupational Exploration	39.95	_____
____	Consultants & Consulting Organizations Directory	545.00	_____
____	Dictionary of Occupational Titles	39.95	_____

___ Directory of Executive Recruiters 1997	44.95	_____
___ Directory of Federal Jobs and Employers	21.95	_____
___ Encyclopedia of Associations 1997	1,149.00	_____
___ Encyclopedia of Careers/Vocational Guidance	149.95	_____
___ _Enhanced_ Guide For Occupational Exploration	34.95	_____
___ Government Phone Book USA 1997	185.00	_____
___ Guide to Internet Databases	114.00	_____
___ **HOOVER'S KEY EMPLOYER DIRECTORIES**	**141.95**	_____
___ ▪ Hoover's 500	29.95	_____
___ ▪ Hoover's Emerging Companies 1996	29.95	_____
___ ▪ Hoover's Guide to Computer Companies	34.95	_____
___ ▪ Hoover's Handbook of World Business	27.95	_____
___ ▪ Hoover's Top 2,500 Employers	22.95	_____
___ Internships 1997	24.95	_____
___ **JOB FINDERS FOR 1997**	**50.95**	_____
___ ▪ Government Job Finder	16.95	_____
___ ▪ Nonprofit's and Education Job Finder	16.95	_____
___ ▪ Professional's Private Sector Job Finder	18.95	_____
___ Job Hunter's Sourcebook	69.95	_____
___ Job Hunter's Yellow Pages	35.00	_____
___ Jobs Rated Almanac	16.95	_____
___ Moving & Relocation Sourcebook	179.95	_____
___ National Job Hotline Directory 1997	14.95	_____
___ National Trade & Professional Associations	85.00	_____
___ Occupational Outlook Handbook	16.95	_____
___ Personnel Executives Contactbook	149.00	_____
___ Professional Careers Sourcebook	99.95	_____
___ Student Access Guide: The Internship Bible	25.00	_____
___ Training & Development Organizations Directory	389.00	_____
___ U.S. Industrial Outlook	29.95	_____
___ Vocational Careers Sourcebook	84.95	_____

City and State Job Banks

___ Job Bank Guide to Employment Services 1996-1997	159.95	_____
___ **METROPOLITAN EMPLOYER CONTACT**		
DIRECTORIES KIT (51 titles)	**873.95**	_____
___ ▪ Atlanta (Job Bank)	16.95	_____
___ ▪ Atlanta (How to Get a Job in)	16.95	_____
___ ▪ Austin/San Antonio (Job Bank)	16.95	_____
___ ▪ Boston (Job Bank)	16.95	_____
___ ▪ Boston & New England (Job Seekers)	15.95	_____
___ ▪ Carolina (Job Bank)	15.95	_____
___ ▪ Cincinnati (Job Bank)	16.95	_____
___ ▪ Chicago (Job Bank)	16.95	_____
___ ▪ Chicago (How to Get a Job in)	16.95	_____
___ ▪ Chicago & Illinois (Job Seekers)	15.95	_____
___ ▪ Chicago Area Companies (Hoover's Guide...)	24.95	_____
___ ▪ Cleveland (Job Bank)	16.95	_____
___ ▪ Dallas/Fort Worth (Job Bank)	16.95	_____
___ ▪ Denver (Job Bank)	15.95	_____

___	■ Detroit (Job Bank)	16.95 ___
___	■ Europe (How to Get a Job in)	17.95 ___
___	■ Florida (Job Bank)	16.95 ___
___	■ Houston (Job Bank)	16.95 ___
___	■ Indianapolis (Job Bank)	16.95 ___
___	■ Las Vegas (Job Bank)	16.95 ___
___	■ Los Angeles (Job Bank)	16.95 ___
___	■ Los Angeles & S. California (Job Seekers)	16.95 ___
___	■ Mid-Atlantic (Job Seekers)	15.95 ___
___	■ Minneapolis/St. Paul (Job Bank)	16.95 ___
___	■ Missouri (Job Bank)	16.95 ___
___	■ Mountain & Plains States (Job Seekers)	15.95 ___
___	■ New Mexico (Job Bank)	16.95 ___
___	■ New York (Job Bank)	16.95 ___
___	■ New York (How to Get a Job in)	16.95 ___
___	■ New York & New Jersey (Job Seekers)	15.95 ___
___	■ New York Area Companies (Hoover's Guide...)	24.95 ___
___	■ North New England (Job Bank)	16.95 ___
___	■ Ohio (Job Bank)	16.95 ___
___	■ Pacific Northwest (Job Seekers)	15.95 ___
___	■ Philadelphia (Job Bank)	16.95 ___
___	■ Phoenix (Job Bank)	15.95 ___
___	■ Pittsburgh (Job Bank)	16.95 ___
___	■ Portland (Job Bank)	16.95 ___
___	■ San Francisco (Job Bank)	16.95 ___
___	■ San Francisco (How to Get a Job in)	16.95 ___
___	■ Seattle (Job Bank)	16.95 ___
___	■ Seattle/Portland (How to Get a Job in)	16.95 ___
___	■ Southern California (How to Get a Job in)	16.95 ___
___	■ Southern California Area Companies (Hoover's...)	24.95 ___
___	■ Southern States (Job Seekers)	15.95 ___
___	■ Southwest (Job Seekers)	15.95 ___
___	■ Tennessee (Job Bank)	16.95 ___
___	■ Texas Area Companies (Hoover's Guide...)	24.95 ___
___	■ Upstate New York (Job Bank)	16.95 ___
___	■ Virginia (Job Bank)	16.95 ___
___	■ Washington, DC (Job Bank)	16.95 ___
___	National Job Bank 1997	294.95 ___

Using the Internet and Computers

___	Be Your Own Headhunter Online	16.00 ___
___	Electronic Job Search Revolution	12.95 ___
___	Electronic Resume Revolution	12.95 ___
___	Electronic Resumes: Putting Your Resume On-Line	19.95 ___
___	Electronic Resumes For the New Job Market	11.95 ___
___	Finding a Job On the Internet	16.95 ___
___	Getting On the Information Superhighway	11.95 ___
___	Guide to Internet Job Searching	14.95 ___
___	Hook Up, Get Hired	12.95 ___
___	How to Get Your Dream Job Using the Internet	29.99 ___

_____ Net Jobs: How to Use the Internet   12.95   _____
_____ On-Line Job Search Companion   16.95   _____
_____ Point and Click Jobfinder   14.95   _____
_____ Selling On the Internet   24.95   _____
_____ Three-Rs of E-Mail   12.95   _____
_____ Using the Internet and the WWW in Your Job Search   16.95   _____
_____ Using WordPerfect In Your Job Search   19.95   _____

Finding Great Jobs and Careers

_____ 100 Best Careers For the 21st Century   15.95   _____
_____ 100 Fastest Growing Companies in America   14.95   _____
_____ 101 Great Answers/Toughest Job Search Problems   11.99   _____
_____ 101 Ways to Power Up Your Job Search   12.95   _____
_____ 110 Biggest Mistakes Job Hunters Make   15.95   _____
_____ 150 Best Companies For Liberal Arts Grads   14.95   _____
_____ 303 Off the Wall Ways to Get a Job   12.99   _____
_____ Adams Jobs Almanac 1997   15.95   _____
_____ Adventure Careers   11.99   _____
_____ American Almanac of Jobs & Salaries   20.00   _____
_____ America's Top Jobs Book Plus CD-ROM   39.95   _____
_____ Best Jobs For the 1990s & Into the 21st Century   19.95   _____
_____ But What If I Don't Want to Go to College   10.95   _____
_____ Career Atlas   12.99   _____
_____ Career Finder   16.00   _____
_____ Career Planning For the 1990s   12.95   _____
_____ Career Success Formula   10.95   _____
_____ Careers For College Majors   32.95   _____
_____ Careers in Computers   17.95   _____
_____ Careers in Education   17.95   _____
_____ Careers in Health Care   17.95   _____
_____ Careers in High Tech   17.95   _____
_____ Careers in Multimedia   24.95   _____
_____ Change Your Job, Change Your Life   17.95   _____
_____ Complete Idiot's Guide to Getting the Job You Want   24.95   _____
_____ Complete Job Finder's Guide to the 90's   13.95   _____
_____ Complete Job Search Handbook   13.95   _____
_____ Crystal-Barkley Career Design Handbook   9.95   _____
_____ Dare to Change Your Job and Your Life   14.95   _____
_____ Directory of Executive Recruiters 1997   44.95   _____
_____ Dynamite Job Finding Skills For the 90's   69.95   _____
_____ End of Work   15.95   _____
_____ Five Secrets to Finding a Job   12.95   _____
_____ Free and Inexpensive Career Materials   19.95   _____
_____ Get a Job You Love!   19.95   _____
_____ Hidden Job Market 1997   18.95   _____
_____ Hi-Tech Jobs For Lo-Tech People   16.95   _____
_____ Hoover's Top 2,500 Employers   22.95   _____
_____ How to Get Interviews From Classified Job Ads   14.95   _____
_____ How to Make Use of a Useless Degree   13.00   _____
_____ How to Strengthen Your Winning Business Personality 11.95   _____

____	How to Succeed Without a Career Path	13.95 ____
____	How You Really Get Hired	11.00 ____
____	In Transition	12.50 ____
____	Job Finding Skills For Smart Dummies	37.95 ____
____	Job Hunter's Word Finder	12.95 ____
____	Job Hunting For Dummies	16.99 ____
____	Job Hunter's Catalog	10.95 ____
____	Jobs 1997	16.00 ____
____	Jobs and Careers With Nonprofit Organizations	15.95 ____
____	Jobs For Lawyers	14.95 ____
____	Jobs Rated Almanac	16.95 ____
____	Joyce Lain Kennedy's Career Book	29.95 ____
____	Knock 'Em Dead 1997	12.95 ____
____	Mid-Career Job Hunting	14.00 ____
____	NBEW's Job Search Books	63.75 ____
____	*New* Complete Guide to Environmental Careers	15.95 ____
____	*New* Relocating Spouse's Guide to Employment	14.95 ____
____	Nonprofits and Education Job Finder	16.95 ____
____	Outdoor Careers	16.95 ____
____	Overnight Job Finder	23.95 ____
____	Part-Time Jobs	32.95 ____
____	Professional's Private Sector Job Finder	18.95 ____
____	Quantum Companies	24.95 ____
____	Rites of Passage at $100,000+	29.95 ____
____	Researching Your Way to a Good Job	14.95 ____
____	Resumes Don't Get Jobs	10.95 ____
____	Top 10 Fears of Job Seekers	12.00 ____
____	Very Quick Job Search	14.95 ____
____	What Color Is Your Parachute? 1997	16.95 ____
____	World Almanac Job Finder's Guide 1997	24.95 ____

Great Jobs and Careers Series

____	**"AMERICA'S TOP JOBS" SERIES**	**134.95** ____
____	▪ 50 Fastest Growing Jobs	14.95 ____
____	▪ Federal Jobs	14.95 ____
____	▪ Top 300 Jobs	18.95 ____
____	▪ Top Jobs For College Graduates	14.95 ____
____	▪ Top Jobs For People Without College	12.95 ____
____	▪ Top Industries	14.95 ____
____	▪ Top Medical and Human Service Jobs	14.95 ____
____	▪ Top Military Jobs	19.95 ____
____	▪ Top Office, Management & Sales Jobs	12.95 ____
____	**"CAREERS IN..." CAREER GUIDANCE SERIES**	**359.95** ____
____	▪ Accounting ('91)	17.95 ____
____	▪ Advertising ('96)	17.95 ____
____	▪ Business ('91)	17.95 ____
____	▪ Child Care ('94)	17.95 ____
____	▪ Communications ('94)	17.95 ____
____	▪ Computers ('95)	17.95 ____
____	▪ Education ('93)	17.95 ____

____	▪ Engineering ('93)	17.95 ____
____	▪ Environment ('95)	17.95 ____
____	▪ Finance ('93)	17.95 ____
____	▪ Government ('94)	17.95 ____
____	▪ Health Care ('95)	17.95 ____
____	▪ High Tech ('92)	17.95 ____
____	▪ Horticulture ('96)	17.95 ____
____	▪ International Business ('96)	17.95 ____
____	▪ Journalism ('95)	17.95 ____
____	▪ Law ('92)	17.95 ____
____	▪ Marketing ('95)	17.95 ____
____	▪ Medicine ('96)	17.95 ____
____	▪ Science ('96)	17.95 ____
____	▪ Social & Rehabilitation Services ('94)	17.95 ____
____	*"CAREERS FOR YOU"* SERIES	359.95 ____
____	▪ Animal Lovers ('91)	14.95 ____
____	▪ Bookworms ('95)	14.95 ____
____	▪ Caring People ('95)	14.95 ____
____	▪ Computer Buffs ('93)	14.95 ____
____	▪ Crafty People ('93)	14.95 ____
____	▪ Culture Lovers ('91)	14.95 ____
____	▪ Environmental Types ('93)	14.95 ____
____	▪ Fashion Plates ('96)	14.95 ____
____	▪ Film Buffs ('93)	14.95 ____
____	▪ Foreign Language Aficionados ('92)	14.95 ____
____	▪ Good Samaritans ('91)	14.95 ____
____	▪ Gourmets ('93)	14.95 ____
____	▪ Health Nuts ('96)	14.95 ____
____	▪ History Buffs ('94)	14.95 ____
____	▪ Kids at Heart ('94)	14.95 ____
____	▪ Music Lovers ('96)	14.95 ____
____	▪ Mystery Lovers ('96)	14.95 ____
____	▪ Nature Lovers ('92)	14.95 ____
____	▪ Night Owl ('95)	14.95 ____
____	▪ Numbers Crunchers ('93)	14.95 ____
____	▪ Plant Lovers ('93)	14.95 ____
____	▪ Shutterbugs ('94)	14.95 ____
____	▪ Sports Nuts ('91)	14.95 ____
____	▪ Travel Buffs ('92)	14.95 ____
____	▪ Writers ('95)	14.95 ____

Cover Letters

____	175 High-Impact Cover Letters	10.95 ____
____	200 Letters for Job Hunters	19.95 ____
____	201 Dynamite Job Search Letters	19.95 ____
____	201 Killer Cover Letters	16.95 ____
____	Adams Cover Letter Almanac and Disk	19.95 ____
____	Cover Letters For Dummies	12.99 ____
____	Cover Letters That Knock 'Em Dead	10.95 ____
____	Dynamite Cover Letters	14.95 ____

___	NBEW's Cover Letters	11.95	___
___	Perfect Cover Letter	9.95	___
___	Sure-Hire Cover Letters	10.95	___

Resumes

___	100 Winning Résumés for $100,000+ Jobs	24.95	___
___	101 Great Résumés	9.99	___
___	101 Résumés for Sure-Hire Results	10.95	___
___	175 High-Impact Résumés	10.95	___
___	Adams Résumé Almanac	10.95	___
___	Asher's Bible of Executive Résumés	29.95	___
___	Best Résumés for $75,000+ Executive Jobs	14.95	___
___	Complete Idiot's Guide to Crafting the Perfect Résumé	16.95	___
___	Designing the Perfect Résumé	12.95	___
___	Dynamite Résumés	14.95	___
___	Dynamite Résumés for $100,000+ Jobs	24.95	___
___	Electronic Résumé Revolution	12.95	___
___	Electronic Résumés: Putting Your Résumé On-Line	19.95	___
___	Electronic Résumés for the New Job Market	11.95	___
___	Encyclopedia of Job-Winning Résumés	16.95	___
___	Gallery of Best Résumés	16.95	___
___	Gallery of Best Résumés for Two-Year Degree Graduates	14.95	___
___	High Impact Résumés and Letters	14.95	___
___	How to Prepare Your Curriculum Vitae	14.95	___
___	NBEW's Résumés	11.95	___
___	New Perfect Résumé	10.95	___
___	Power Résumés	12.95	___
___	Quick Résumé and Cover Letter Book	9.95	___
___	Real-Life Résumés That Work!	12.95	___
___	Résumé Catalog	15.95	___
___	Résumé Kit	9.95	___
___	Résumé Pro	24.95	___
___	Résumé Shortcuts	14.95	___
___	Résumé Solution	12.95	___
___	Résumés for Advertising Careers	9.95	___
___	Résumés for Architecture and Related Careers	9.95	___
___	Résumés for Banking and Financial Careers	9.95	___
___	Résumés for Business Management Careers	9.95	___
___	Résumés for College Students and Recent Graduates	9.95	___
___	Résumés for Communications Careers	9.95	___
___	Résumés for Dummies	12.99	___
___	Résumés for Education Careers	9.95	___
___	Résumés for Engineering Careers	9.95	___
___	Résumés for Environmental Careers	9.95	___
___	Résumés for Ex-Military Personnel	9.95	___
___	Résumés for 50+ Job Hunters	9.95	___
___	Résumés for First-Time Job Hunter	9.95	___
___	Résumés for the Healthcare Professional	12.95	___
___	Résumés for High School Graduates	9.95	___
___	Résumés for High Tech Careers	9.95	___

___ Résumés for Midcareer Job Changers	9.95	___
___ Résumés for the Over 50 Job Hunter	14.95	___
___ Résumés for Re-Entering the Job Market	9.95	___
___ Résumés for Sales and Marketing Careers	9.95	___
___ Résumés for Scientific and Technical Careers	9.95	___
___ Résumés That Knock 'Em Dead	10.95	___
___ Résumés, Résumés, Résumés	9.99	___
___ Smart Woman's Guide to Résumés & Job Hunting	9.95	___
___ Sure-Hire Résumés	14.95	___

Skills, Testing, Self-Assessment, Empowerment

___ 7 Habits of Highly Effective People	14.00	___
___ Career Satisfaction and Success	9.95	___
___ Chicken Soup for the Soul	12.95	___
___ Discover the Best Jobs for You	11.95	___
___ Do What You Are	14.95	___
___ Do What You Love, the Money Will Follow	10.95	___
___ Love Your Work and Success Will Follow	12.95	___
___ P.I.E. Method for Career Success	14.95	___

Dress and Etiquette

___ 110 Mistakes Working Women Make...	9.95	___
___ Dress Casually For Success . ... For Men	16.95	___
___ Executive Etiquette in the New Workplace	14.95	___
___ John Molloy's New Dress For Success (Men)	13.99	___
___ *New* Women's Dress For Success	12.99	___
___ Red Socks Don't Work!	14.95	___
___ Winning Image	17.95	___

Networking and Power Building

___ Dynamite Networking For Dynamite Jobs	15.95	___
___ Dynamite Tele-Search	12.95	___
___ Great Connections	19.95	___
___ How to Work a Room	11.99	___
___ NBEW's Networking	10.95	___
___ Network Your Way to Success	19.95	___
___ Network Your Way to Your Next Job	14.95	___
___ Power Networking	14.95	___
___ Power Schmoozing	12.95	___
___ Power to Get In	24.95	___
___ Secrets of Savvy Networking	12.99	___

Interviewing

___ 50 Winning Answers to Interview Questions	10.95	___
___ 60 Seconds and You're Hired	9.95	___
___ 90-Minute Interview Prep Book	15.95	___

___ 101 Dynamite Questions to Ask at Your Job Interview	14.95	___
___ 101 Great Answers/Interview Questions	9.99	___
___ 111 Dynamite Ways to Ace Your Job Interview	13.95	___
___ Adams Job Interview Almanac	10.95	___
___ Best Answers to 201 Most/Asked Interview Questions	10.95	___
___ Conquer Interview Objections	10.95	___
___ Dynamite Answers to Interview Questions	11.95	___
___ Dynamite Salary Negotiations	13.95	___
___ Interview For Success	15.95	___
___ Interview Kit	10.95	___
___ Interview Power	12.95	___
___ Job Interviews For Dummies	12.99	___
___ Killer Interviews	10.95	___
___ Naked At the Interview	10.95	___
___ NBEW's Interviewing	11.95	___
___ Perfect Follow-Up Method to Win the Job	12.95	___
___ Power Interviews	12.95	___
___ Quick Interview and Salary Negotiation Book	12.95	___
___ Sweaty Palms	8.95	___

Military and Spouses

___ Becoming a Better Leader and Getting Promoted in Today's Army	13.95	___
___ Beyond the Uniform	14.95	___
___ Complete Guide to the NCO-ER	13.95	___
___ **CORPORATE GRAY SERIES**	**51.95**	___
___ ▪ From Air Force Blue to Corporate Gray	17.95	___
___ ▪ From Army Green to Corporate Gray	17.95	___
___ ▪ From Navy Blue to Corporate Gray	17.95	___
___ Guide to Civilian Jobs For Enlisted Naval Personnel	14.95	___
___ Job Search: Marketing Your Military Experience	16.95	___
___ Jobs and the Military Spouse	14.95	___
___ New Relocating Spouse's Guide/Employment	14.95	___
___ Out of Uniform	12.95	___
___ Retiring From the Military	25.95	___
___ Today's Military Wife	16.95	___
___ Up or Out: How to Get Promoted/Army Draws Down	13.95	___

Government

___ Book of U.S. Postal Exams	17.95	___
___ Complete Guide to Public Employment	19.95	___
___ Directory of Federal Jobs and Employers	21.95	___
___ Federal Application Kit	56.95	___
___ Federal Applications That Get Results	23.95	___
___ Federal Jobs in Law Enforcement	14.95	___
___ Federal Resume Guidebook	34.95	___
___ Find a Federal Job Fast!	15.95	___
___ Government Job Finder	16.95	___

Law and Paralegal Careers

___	Best Resumes For Attorneys	16.95	___
___	Careers in Law	17.95	___
___	Jobs For Lawyers	14.95	___
___	Paralegal	11.95	___
___	Paralegal Career Guide	24.95	___

Women

___	110 Mistakes Working Women Make....	9.95	___
___	Big Book of Opportunities For Women	39.95	___
___	Every Woman's Essential Job Hunting /Resume Book	10.95	___
___	Job/Family Challenge	12.95	___
___	More Power to You	10.99	___
___	National Directory/Women-Owned Business Firms	279.00	___
___	*New* Women's Dress For Success	12.99	___
___	Resumes For Re-Entry	10.95	___
___	**SMART WOMAN'S SUCCESS GUIDES**	**47.95**	___
___	▪ Smart Woman's Guide /Career Success	11.95	___
___	▪ Smart Woman's Guide/Interviewing & Salary Neg.	12.99	___
___	▪ Smart Woman's Guide /Resumes & Job Hunting	9.99	___
___	▪ Smart Woman's Guide /Starting a Business	14.95	___
___	Smart Women, Smart Moves	19.95	___
___	Survival Guide For Women	16.95	___
___	Surviving Your Partner's Job Loss	12.95	___
___	Taking Charge	14.95	___
___	Ten Stupid Things Women Do to Mess Up Their Lives	10.95	___
___	Woman Source Catalog and Review	19.95	___
___	Women and Risk	19.95	___
___	You Just Don't Understand	12.95	___

Minorities and Special Needs Groups

___	Best Companies For Minorities	12.95	___
___	Big Book of Minority Opportunities	39.95	___
___	Black Student's Guide to Colleges	19.95	___
___	Black Student's Guide to Scholarships	14.95	___
___	Career Success For People With Physical Disabilities	16.95	___
___	College & Career Success/Learning Disabilities	14.95	___
___	Financial Aid For Minority Students	29.95	___
___	Job Strategies For People With Disabilities	14.95	___
___	Minority Career Guide	12.95	___
___	Minority Career Handbook	9.95	___
___	National Directory of Minority Opportunities	49.95	___
___	National Directory/Minority-Owned Business Firms	279.00	___
___	Peterson's Colleges/Students/Learning Disabilities	26.95	___
___	Successful Job Search Strategies For the Disabled	14.95	___
___	Why Should White Guys Have All the Fun?	22.95	___
___	Work, Sister, Work	19.95	___

Entrepreneurs, Self Employment, Consultants

____ 10 Hottest Consulting Practices	27.95	_____
____ 101 Best Businesses to Start	17.50	_____
____ Adams Businesses You Can Start Almanac	14.95	_____
____ Adams Streetwise Small Business Start-Up	16.95	_____
____ Best Home-Based Businesses For the 90s	12.95	_____
____ Finding Your Perfect Work	16.95	_____
____ Franchise Opportunities Handbook	16.95	_____
____ How to Build a Successful One-Person Business	25.95	_____

SUBTOTAL _____

Virginia residents add 4½% sales tax _____

POSTAGE/HANDLING ($4.00 for first
title and $1.50 for each additional book) $4.00

Number of additional titles x $1.50---------------- _____

TOTAL ENCLOSED -------------------- _____

SHIP TO:

NAME _____

ADDRESS _____

_____

❑ I enclose check/moneyorder for $ _____ made payable to
IMPACT PUBLICATIONS.

❑ Please charge $ _____ to my credit card:

❑ Visa   ❑ MasterCard   ❑ American Express

Card # _____

Expiration date: _____ / _____

Signature _____

We accept official purchase orders from libraries, educational institutions, and
government offices. Please attach copy with official signature(s).

The On-Line Superstore & Warehouse

Hundreds of Terrific Career Resources Conveniently Available On the World Wide Web 24-Hours a Day, 365 Days a Year!

Ever wanted to know what are the newest and best books, directories, newsletters, wall charts, training programs, videos, CD-ROMs, computer software, and kits available to help you land a job, negotiate a higher salary, or start your own business? What about finding a job in Asia or relocating to San Francisco? Are you curious about how to find a job 24-hours a day by using the Internet or what to do after you leave the military? Trying to keep up-to-date on the latest career resources but not able to find the latest catalogs, brochures, or newsletters on today's "best of the best" resources?

Welcome to the first virtual career bookstore on the Internet. Now you're only a "click" away with Impact Publication's electronic solution to the resource challenge. Impact Publications, one of the nation's leading publishers and distributors of career resources, has launched its comprehensive "Career Superstore and Warehouse" on the Internet. The bookstore is jam-packed with the latest resources focusing on several key career areas:

- Alternative jobs and careers
- Self-assessment
- Career planning and job search
- Employers
- Relocation and cities
- Resumes
- Cover Letters
- Dress, image, and etiquette
- Education
- Telephone
- Military
- Salaries
- Interviewing
- Nonprofits

- Empowerment
- Self-esteem
- Goal setting
- Executive recruiters
- Entrepreneurship
- Government
- Networking
- Electronic job search
- International jobs
- Travel
- Law
- Training and presentations
- Minorities
- Physically challenged

"This is more than just a bookstore offering lots of product," say Drs. Ron and Caryl Krannich, two of the nation's leading career experts and authors and developers of this on-line bookstore. *"We're an important resource center for libraries, corporations, government, educators, trainers, and career counselors who are constantly defining and redefining this dynamic field. Of the thousands of career resources we review each year, we only select the 'best of the best.'"*

Visit this rich site and you'll quickly discover just about everything you ever wanted to know about finding jobs, changing careers, and starting your own business—including many useful resources that are difficult to find in local bookstores and libraries. The site also includes what's new and hot, tips for job search success, and monthly specials. Impact's Web address is:

http://www.impactpublications.com